Rock and Roll and UFOs

Gregg Kofi Brown

Typeset by Jonathan Downes,
Cover by Martin Cook; Layout by SPiderKaT for CFZ Communications
Using Microsoft Word 2000, Microsoft Publisher 2000, Adobe Photoshop CS.

First published in Great Britain by Gonzo Multimedia

c/o Brooks City,
6th Floor New Baltic House
65 Fenchurch Street,
London EC3M 4BE
Fax: +44 (0)191 5121104
Tel: +44 (0) 191 5849144
International Numbers:
Germany: Freephone 08000 825 699
USA: Freephone 18666 747 289

© Gonzo Multimedia MMXVi

All rights reserved. Without limiting the rights under copyright reserved above, no part of this publication may be reproduced, stored in or introduced into a retrieval system, or transmitted, in any form of by any means (electronic, mechanical, photocopying, recording or otherwise), without the prior written permission of both the copyright owners and the publishers of this book.

ISBN 978-1-908728-60-9

Contents

Preface	5
Chapter 1 .. Beginning the Journey	7
Chapter 2 .. North to Alaska	15
Chapter 3 .. LA Rock!	23
Chapter 4 .. Something in the Desert Sky	33
Chapter 5 .. London Calling	45
Chapter 6 .. African Vibes	81
Chapter 7 .. Number 1 in the America!	87
Chapter 8 .. Life Changes	95
Chapter 9 .. Black to Africa	103
Chapter 10 .. Rock Opera	113
Epilogue .. A Better World	123

Preface

My life in the music and entertainment industry has always had its entry point on several cascading levels. That is to say that, the various opportunities that have availed themselves to me has forced me to wear many hats on a daily basis. Whether it's supporting Jimmy Cliff at a festival in Vienna or teaching a music theory class in London, I am blessed to be working in a business I enjoy.

Having a broad interest in the technical and practical side of music has embedded me with skills that have extended my nocturnal shelf life to the point where I still have an active career. With the current trends and challenges in the industry such as downloading, You Tube and social media, one is amazed that the ability to eek out a living is still plausible in this ever changing, landscape.

However there are constants that remain as basic building blocks within the realm of popular music currency such as publishing, performing rights, recording agreements, marketing/PR, merchandising, performance income and production.

So basically it does not matter what type of challenges the music business is going through, in order to have longevity in this or any industry you should have a solid foundation upon which to base a career.

From the outset at the start of any career you generally start in an ensemble whether it's playing flute in an orchestra or singing harmony on a street corner with your mates. There are solo artists that are exceptions to the rule and exceptionally gifted.

However most of us normal people have to work very hard to develop our craft and then work very hard to maintain it. My story is probably similar to many who have ended up in the music world. From humble beginnings in a choir or an orchestra…to something you could do well and with a bit of effort be impressive.

Then you discover pop music and try to integrate that into your classical or secular mode of music. Well it took me a long time to figure that one out. I grew up during the end, of segregation in America where everything had to fit into a box…even music…at first.

But as I played in orchestra & sang in madrigals I found myself jamming with friends playing a song by The Stones or getting down on the funk with James Brown. Thus I began to codify music and culture through education, social intercourse, political awareness, performance and practice. By the time I was asked to produce a tribute album, for Damilola Taylor, the ten year old Nigerian boy, who was murdered in South East London, I had enough life and professional experience to make it happen. That and a bit of luck enabled me to enlist the rock & pop artists of the day and negotiate clearances with the record companies.

I have met so many students who say they are producers or performers and they know nothing about music theory. Some of them are amazing at what they do at that given time, in that given circumstance and in that specific genre but what if it all changes?

I want my readers to be aware of the magic that happens in this business. There is a mystical element to being creative and the influence this creativity can have on ordinary lives is amazing. I even talk about the UFO experience I had on the way to a gig. I have rarely ever mentioned that event to anyone but I reveal it here and most of my friends will never have heard about the incident. To tell the truth I am not here to make myself look good bad or indifferent.

I will just present the facts, some of which leads to success and others that lead me nowhere. I include my mistakes, which I point out and the alternative route I might have taken. My knowledge of the music business was gained mostly through practical experience, as they did not really teach this as a subject at very many universities in the 70s.

Of course music composition and music theory courses were a gateway into music academia and research…it is even good for those wanting to be arrangers & producers. But how do you teach someone to write a hit song? Bottom line is you can't but you can describe the process and the conditions that may lead to you writing a hit.

I look at the vast array of talent I have been very blessed to have worked with and observe what they needed from me as an artist and what I gained from them artistically. Whether it's trying to get a bass feel in the middle of a jam with Damon Albarn at an *African Express* gig or learning that *Guns n Roses* bought the rights to songs I have publishing on.

I will present these scenarios and snippets from that side of my life as examples of a career practice gone good or bad. Having had a number one record in America as a songwriter, starred in several London West end musical hits and toured the world with the legend that is *Osibisa*, I have earned the respect of my peers as a musician. Once we get past my initial humble beginnings… the scenarios will present themselves as I move from one career decision to another from booking Elton John to turning down a gig with Johnny Guitar Watson to playing to one hundred thousand people at a festival with Joe Cocker.

These snippets of music business narrative can be used as a guide in the great big world of a freelance artist operating in the music universe or give a reader on holiday a fly on the wall view of the entertainment business.

Chapter 1
Beginning the journey

I was born at John Gatson Hospital in Memphis, Tennessee. The earliest thing I can remember seeing is my grandmother braiding her hair. Church played a big part in our lives so you could find us there every Sunday. The choir was amazing with their harmonies although a bit scary to a 4 year old.

My cousin eventually took over as pastor of the local church. I had so many cousins in Memphis it was crazy. My mother's first cousin on my grandma's side, were to have the biggest influence on my life. They even had a piano which I was allowed to tickle every now and then.

But singing with Cousin Ann's sons: Mose, Guy, Ray, Dewy and Junior kept me in good stead for the future. They were not just good crooners, they were amazing at American football. This meant I had to at least make the team even if I sat on the bench which I did. So by the time I got to my senior year I sang in Madrigals and played on the varsity football squad.

My upbringing was a bit chaotic... my mum took me to LA when I was 2years old but, sent me and my newly borne sister Stephanie back to Memphis to be cared for by my Grandma.

Then out of the blue my mum shows up in Memphis newly married again and pregnant with her third child. She then takes my sister Stephanie and I up to Anchorage, Alaska. We stayed there for two years then moved to Riverside, California by way of Memphis.

So one year I'd be in Memphis and the next year in Southern California... this happened until I was 17 when I graduated from Riverside Polytechnic High School in California. My time in Memphis was spent mainly singing doing homework and playing football.

My time in California was spent mainly singing doing homework and playing football. It sounds the same but there were differences in how they played football in Memphis and how they played football in California. Memphis players had way better technique and stamina than the California teams.

And the music... well lets just say that in California we had *The Beatles*, The Stones, Elvis,

Jan & Dean, Dick Dale and the *Beach Boys*. In Memphis we had *The Beatles, The Stones,* Elvis, BB King, Howling Wolf, *The Staple Singers*, Rufus Thomas, Otis Redding, Sonny Terry and Brownie McGhee.

But hey…I embraced all of these cultural nuances and having a stepfather who was a jazz musician for a while added another colour to my musical palette. So my junior year (year 11) in Memphis saw me go to the prom with my 3rd cousin and her sister who the dated the captain of the football team.

We were suited and booted in a convertible Cadillac and none other than the *Bar Kays* (Otis Redding's backing band) were playing. Although I had a hotter date, who was not a relative, for my senior prom in California the band weren't nearly as hot as the *Bar Kays*. Sadly they (*Bar Kays*) perished with Otis Redding in a plane crash the year of my senior prom.

Now an interesting point: In my junior year in Memphis I was offered $27,000 worth of scholarships from 5 different colleges… a lot of money in those days. But my senior year brought an offer from the prestigious Chapman College, City of Orange, California, however I blew that opportunity…the details of which I won't go into. Sufficient to say I ended up at my local college in Riverside and attended the University of California at Riverside. I started jamming on the bass when I was 15 so at 17, I formed a funk band with some local kids playing James Brown mostly.

The band had horns; I fronted it and played bass on a couple numbers. We used to play at community events, school dances such as the prom at my ole high school. I was a stronger singer than bass player in those days but that would change in time.

I think most of my time early on in music was spent with these mad choirmasters especially in catholic schools where we would sing Latin for hours guided by the Holy Sisters of the winding sheet. In Memphis our high school Choir Director was the great Omar Robinson who was amazing, and often arranged vocals for Stax Records!

At 12 in California I played cello then moved on to upright bass however when I moved to Memphis the school did not have an orchestra only a marching band and a choir. This was hard as I lost my reading chops on bass and although I tried to get back into it when I returned to California it wasn't the same.

Stepfather number 2 Arthur James Theus was a jazz musician known as 'Fats Theus' he is the father of my youngest brother AJ. Fats played with Jimmy McGriff and wrote a minor hit for him called 'The Worm' which was sampled on a recent Chemical Brothers track a few years ago.

Fats led his own trio in between dates with McGriff, it was very cool and sometimes he would play locally! We had a Hammond B3 in the house, and the drummer, Al Wilson lived in the flat we had on the top floor of our house. Al would later become a star in his own right with his hits 'The Snake' and 'Show and Tell'.

Al was a very focused man. He practiced martial arts in the front yard, and had some very beautiful girlfriends. The jazz they played was not my cup of tea but the music had an effect on me subconsciously and would rear its ugly head at various times in my career.

My mum was a bit of an entrepreneur who had a successful beauty shop. There was a lot of jealousy for mum as she was very popular and her business boasted black, white and Latino clients. When mysteriously the lease was not renewed… she carried on doing hair at our house. Mum promoted gigs and had a nite club for a while she co-owned with Charlie Cook… the most amazing cook on the west coast. After a show sometimes she would have parties at our house and the food was always superb!

With all the eclectic music around my life…jazz at home… classical at school I gravitated towards pop, rock and soul music. The first single I bought at the age of 14 was 'Satisfaction' by the *Rolling Stones*. I heard the song on the radio in my friend's car on the way home from school, I asked his dad to stop the car and I jumped out and went straight to the record shop got the 45 single then walked home. If that's not passion then I don't know what is.

So the duality of my upbringing was sometimes confusing but very rich culturally. California provided a musical experience from a middle class perspective with access to classical, jazz, pop and rock. However, when I lived in Memphis, my grandparents were dirt poor, and my experience, was driven by gospel, blues and soul music. Church played a big part in supporting our spiritual economy… life was tough and it was important to be focused, incorporate and with an indomitable will, and exude the qualities of a southern gentleman.

All the time I was trying to balance being a jock (football), singing in madrigals and choir. This was normal in Memphis as my cousins sang in the school choir and played football but in California it was considered a bit weird. Being in choir was considered nerdy however everyone yearned to be on the football team. I did both I was an oddball… the guys thought I was strange… but the girls loved it.

After graduating from Polytechnic High school I went to summer school at RCC (Riverside City College) where I took a physics course and a computer science class. I then took time out from my studies & got a job working on a new passenger jet plane called a Boeing 747.

Drilling and riveting inside the shell that fits over the jet engine and putting parts of the tail section together with metal bonding was a pretty mundane activity to me. When they offered to pay for me to do an engineering degree I was completely taken aback! Apparently I had scored quite high on the aptitude test but I was adamant about starting my music degree at college.

In my spare time I started jamming with my friends playing some bass and singing.

As I became more confident as a singer I was enlisted by a young guitarist named Gregg Schaffer who played in a band called *Bacon Fat*. They had toured England and made an album with *Mike Vernon* the legendary British producer.

Vernon had produced *John Mayall's Blues Breakers, Fleetwood Mac, Ten Years After*, David Bowie, Champion Jack Dupree and he would go on to produce *Bloodstone, Dexy's Midnight Runners, Level 42* and *The Pasadena's*. Mike Vernon loved Gregg Schaffer's guitar playing and used him on many blues recording sessions with Buddy Reed, J.D Nicholson, Pee Wee Crayton and George Harmonica Smith.

Gregg and I were booked as a duo for a wedding gig with Schaffer on guitar and me on vocals. On the eve of the wedding I went out with this really gorgeous surfer girl, she offered me some pills, which I was not into doing initially. However I wanted to impress her so I took a couple.

We got pulled over by the police. Well I was driving ten miles per hour on a freeway! It was quite embarrassing for me… trying to be cool, and not really handling the situation. In the end I went to jail and she went home. Luckily the wedding was for the daughter of a prominent doctor so he pulled some strings and got me out of jail so I could make the gig. Gregg and I were tight and decided to put a band together.

We linked up with a bassist named Gregg (three Greggs in one band) and a drummer named Mark. We played a couple of warm up gigs… one gig was at Timothy Leary's ranch near Idyllwild California up in the San Jacinto Mountain's. However on the eve of our first festival gig Gregg the bass player died! He had taken some pills to sleep but threw up in his sleep and suffocated.

Gregg Schaffer was never the same after that. I went back to college as planned. About two years later I heard that Gregg Schaffer had been murdered by, the drummer, Mark. It was a tragic end to an amazing talent.

My childhood friend Sedrick Jackson had a piano and played guitar so we used jam at his mom's place all the time. This was a great learning experience for me as well as going to the local beer garden, which was part of the chitlin circuit black musicians played at through out America. There were always serious musicians in these places and usually the best BBQ ribs in town.

One young guitarist whom I used to baby sit named Trey Stone, had a great setup at his mom's house with amps, keyboard, PA and guitars. He was the best musician of all of us who knew and played with the best musicians in the area.

Trey ended up playing guitar for legendary Motown producer Norman Whitfield on records by *Rose Royce* (Carwash) and *Undisputed Truth*. Trey Stone became Bootsy Collins' right hand man on guitar and keyboards… they also backed and recorded with *Deee'lite* on 'Groove is in the Heart'.

The summer before I went back to college I fell out with my mum and moved my things into the garage of a house we owned next door. That garage became my woodshed… I slept there and practised in the heat all day long. I knew I was getting better when my Mum told me to turn down my stereo!

I said it was me... not the stereo and she was blown away. Learning blues, soul, Leon Russell and *Beatles* songs on guitar really helped to set me up as a songwriter. This gave me an abundance of melodic currency and increased my knowledge of chord progressions. I'm grateful for that time in the garage... or the woodshed as we musicians say.

In college I took a split major; Music & African Studies, which I felt would empower me as the teacher I wanted to become. There was a lot of black consciousness in the air at the time, which led to solidarity with Latinos, Anglos, socialists, communists and anyone who expressed equality and unity for all peoples.

It was difficult not to be political. It was around this time I met people associated with the Socialist, Black Panther and Communist parties through my friend David Wood who came from a very political family. He gave me Mao Tse Tung's *Little Red Book* and along with the *Autobiography of Malcolm X* my foray into the political dogma at the time was set.

Almost instantly the cultural and political economy of my life put me into some interesting situations. One of those being, that I was involved in helping to organise a march against the Vietnam War. Over 100,000 people attended this event making it the second largest march against the Vietnam War in the US organised by black students.

This got me on the FBI list for their investigation into the activities of politically aware students on college campuses. I remember my Mum telling me the police came by to tell her that I was seen in the company of communist sympathizers. Reagan was governor of California at the time. He and Nixon were working overtime to vilify those working against the interest and tyranny of corporate America.

The war was never about freedom it was about Dow chemicals and Coca Cola. Everyone knew this and had enough of the body bags with young soldiers and the war machine inflicting suffering on a people who certainly never did any harm to anyone in the black community or white community for that matter.

So my time at college got off to a great start. I took the first job I was offered... a janitor part time... cleaning the student union recreation area. I was proud to be working my way through college although some students may have pointed their finger to make fun. It was good for people to see me as a hard working student.

I caught the attention of Jim who was student body president. His girlfriend Patricia Thibodeaux was Creole and beautiful, we had gone to junior high together. I don't know what she said to him about me but he offered me the position of entertainment director for the college!! Suddenly I had a budget, a secretary, an office and a better job... at the student bookstore.

Like I said it was important for people to see me as a hard working student. As the

Rock and Roll and UFOs

entertainment director I was in charge of student social events, concerts and films. It was a position tailored for my aspirations and abilities. I learnt so much about the entertainment business and it was a post I would keep for 3 years.

One of the first gigs I produced was Elton John's first proper concert in the USA. Before then he had only played small clubs like the Troubadour in Los Angeles but I knew his star was on the rise. So when I was given the opportunity to put him on as a favour to his agency Chartwell I jumped at the chance.

Chartwell Artists wanted £1500.00 for Elton John, which was a low fee even for that time. I was being handed an opportunity… It was a no-brainer and he would be commanding ten times that amount within weeks. Even the big boys at the university wanted to get involved.

We had production meetings at an amazing house in Big Bear Mountains. It was a beautiful setting from which to organise the logistics of the event. By letting the University radio jocks get involved I cemented my position at the university before I even enrolled there.

As I looked out over San Bernadino from the vantage point on top of this mountain I felt my social currency was on the rise. Surrounded by like minded, intelligent individuals we all shared the optimistic view that in our time we could make a change from the greed and corruption the US military industrial complex was dictating from its political vantage point.

I was promised a scholarship, a teaching assistant job and a radio spot on KUCR the University of California at Riverside's radio station. As the entertainment director the responsibility of the event lied on my shoulders. As the job was not paid the only money I made was from under the table - deals done with the PA Company and from the agents wanting their acts to support Elton John.

It took a lot of time to organise everything as the gig was to take place in three weeks time. This is normally impossible but we could guarantee a sell out crowd just from the student populations of both the college and the University. We made 5 posters and got adverts on KUCR… the gig sold out in a week and we were getting calls from movie star agents in order to get their clients on the guest list for the gig.

One of the music agents I worked with was Bill Trout who was a paraplegic… paralyzed from the neck down… but he had a team of people at his command and was a very efficient agent. He would become the agent for my bands a few years later.

Bill asked if some Vietnam War veterans, who were all disabled could make a bootleg album of the concert. The idea being they would smuggle a tape machine in one of their wheel chairs. I didn't hesitate to say yes as all the money would go to them and their buddies.

Elton John still lists the bootleg album *Country Comforts* on his discography but they say it was recorded in Santa Monica but it was actually his first big concert in Riverside. You can hear my voice at the end of the gig saying 'ladies and gentlemen Elton John'.

It was an amazing gig! Elton played piano with a drummer and a bassist completing the trio. They rocked the whole place... he must have played 2 ½ to 3 hours. The whole event must have been 4 ½ hours... with the support acts it was like a mini festival.

The next day the assistant Dean came up to me and congratulated me for organising such a great event. He also said he did not mind the students smoking those funny smelling cigarettes but did they have to put them out on the carpet of the auditorium. My life would be set for the next 3 ½ years... anything I wanted I got.

However the gig did not go down well with the Black Student Union. I reasoned with them by saying now that I have proven myself with the powers that be with the Elton John concert this would empower me to do additional gigs with music acts of colour, which I did.

My friend George Quant introduced me to jazz artist Horace Tapscott and we setup weekly workshops and seminars with his jazz Archestra, which included sax icon Black Arthur Blythe. When Horace invited jazz legend Roland Kirk to the workshop we had to move to the student auditorium as the audience suddenly quadrupled in size.

However when I was on my way to the event a woman with a flat tire flagged me down to help change the tire for her... and her passenger was none other than Roland Kirk himself. They were on their way to the gig! Talk about synchronicity.

With the Black Power movement in full swing on college campuses in America I found myself constantly treading on a tightrope between the establishment and the students. The radical white kids, the Chicano movement, black students and the general student population... they all had to be catered for. However I had to reflect the social consciousness of the time.

I still got the odd Uncle Tom jibe but it didn't bother me because people who actually knew me knew where I was really coming from. I immediately set into place a cultural mix of events that catered to all the students at the college. I must have done a good job... I held the post for 3 years, as it was an appointed position, not an elected one.

Chapter 2
North to Alaska

After I moved on to University I met and started jamming with Woody Diaz who was politically active and a grad student at the university I met him through Jeannie Hostetler. I had met Jeannie through political contacts who, were linked with the Peace and Freedom Party. Woody was very intelligent a great percussionist and he was seeing Jeannie. They would end up married with 4 kids.

Woody and I talked about jamming some African Latin rhythms. I was really into *Osibisa, Santana, Mandrill, Cymande*, Tito Puente, Hugh Masekela, Mongo Santamaria, and Antonio Carlos Jobim and so was he. But as a New York Puerto Rican he then introduced me to Willie Colon, Ray Barretto, Celia Cruz, Eddie Palmieri, Johnny Pacheco and Rueben Blades.

Woody then introduced me to brothers Steve and Tony Campbell whose father was a minister of the African Methodist Church. Steve was the drummer & Tony was the guitarist they were a very tight rhythm section.

Now I had my job cut out for me! The brothers were a lot more experienced than me even though they were younger. I was still a university student with a new job as an assistant teacher for the African Studies department and I was given a radio show on the student station so I had a lot on my plate. No I didn't' get out much but I was determined to hold up my end on bass as Tony shared lead vocals with me.

We started doing a few gigs then somehow we got a support slot for a concert at the University. I think it was Woody who got the contact but it was to play a gig supporting *Malo* a Latin rock big band fronted by Jorge Santana, Carlos's brother.

Azteca who were a Latino band fronted by the Escovedo brothers, Pete & Coke, were the main support act. They had made their name playing for Carlos Santana. Pete's young daughter was playing conga, she was amazing and would go on to be known as Sheila E of Prince fame.

Our band *Shango* fit the bill perfectly with our Afro Latin blues sound. The University hosted some amazing concerts during this time. It was where I first saw the original *Osibisa*...and who knew I would be a member of this iconic band 10 years later? Other acts I saw there were *Return to Forever*, Freddie King, *The Allman Brothers*, and Buddy Guy' to name just a few.

I was summarily invited by my best friend Sedrick Jackson to go to Alaska to join a band for the summer. This would be a great opportunity to improve my playing ability. Once I got there, I bought an upright bass & some jazz records and started wood-shedding (practicing). I stayed in Sedrick's dad's office, which was a log cabin with a bedroom at the back.

I forgot how beautiful and wild the Alaskan landscape was. Anchorage sitting on the mouth of an inlet, with the majestic Mount McKinley mountain range as a backdrop was a stunning sight. There were lots of hills and valleys.

I lived in Nunaka Valley, a suburb of Anchorage, when I aged five to seven. The slope of a hill was near the back of our house and us kids used to go sledding down it. I was pretty good at ice-skating back then to… when I was seven.

My partying lifestyle was a bit too much for Sedrick's dad Mr Jackson so I moved in temporarily with Sedrick and his girlfriend Barbara. He had gotten Barbara pregnant so young Sedrick had a lot on his mind. But he still came and went like a single man. One night I came in from a club a bit tipsy and made up my bed on their couch like I would normally do. I got in bed and dozed off…

Next thing I hear is a loud pop like a glass is breaking and I woke up to see a flame coming right for me! It was like someone with a giant flame-thrower. I was in my underwear but I got up and ran screaming outside Fire! Fire! Help! Help!

The neighbours came to our aid, poor Barbara was still up in the bedroom and she was three months pregnant. As she yelled my name Barbara slid down the roof but I didn't get there in time to catch her and she landed on the ground. The fire engines came, as did the ambulance.

The paramedics checked her for injuries then put Barbara on to the gurney and wheeled her to the ambulance. Word was she had minor injuries but they could be long term. The firemen put out the fire, which was of an electrical nature, caused by faulty wiring…this was their prognosis.

I went into the house to put on some clothing when the fire engine left. Then Sedrick comes in through the kitchen…he is so stoned he barely notices the kitchen has been gutted by a fire. I told him what happened and he just said "bummer!" We went to the hospital to see how Barbara was… she was in pain but generally she was ok.

It was great to meet people I went to school with in Anchorage when I was 5-7 years of age. I made some good friends up there. The band Sedrick and I put together was mainly for practice although we did a few gigs and a TV show, where we played original compositions. Hanging out on their little club scene was great. There were some amazing bands that came up and played the hotels in Anchorage. Some great funk bands too!

Rock and Roll and UFOs

We were invited play a local festival in Anchorage complete with mooseburgers and the Lt Governor at the time even got on stage and sang with us. Time was running out for me though I had to get back to University as I only had one year to go. When I checked my bank account…boy did I get a shock! I had run out of money!

Sedrick was lucky to be given money from some local working girls so he went back to LA. Suddenly I was stuck in Alaska! Kenny Blackwell the sax and flute player in the band let me move into his apartment to share the rent. I needed some money fast as winter was approaching and I was in Alaska.

There was a fire 500 miles north of Fairbanks and they needed a mop up crew to work with the fire fighters. Pay was $100 a day. Fine. I thought I'd go for a week and I would be in sunny southern California before the snow. I didn't' know what to expect but when they started instructing us on what to do if attacked by wild bears I started thinking maybe this isn't such a good idea.

Then they explained how we should poke the ground as we walked on the tundra because the fires still burned underground and you could fall into an inferno. However nothing prepared me for the mosquitoes…I mean they could be pretty bad in Memphis being on the banks of a river. But this was mosquito city and I don't seem to recall we had any tents just some heavy tarpaulin to throw over our heads.

So forget about the fact there were no weapons to protect us against wild bears and the idea of falling into a fiery underground furnace I could just about deal with this! But the mosquitoes…no way I could do this for any amount of money.

So, the next day, a mate and I decided to throw in the towel. We were offered a ride back to Anchorage in a mail plane. I'll never forget that flight, with the Alaskan landscape jumping out at us and herds of thousands of reindeer heading south.

It reminded me of the long drive we did from Anchorage to Memphis when I was 7 years old. We hit the Alcan Highway going from Alaska into Canada and I remember the herds of reindeer crossing the highway. The pilot of the mail plane was a nice chap he even offered us a chance to take over the controls of the plane…but that was a no thanks.

When I got back to Anchorage Kenny got me a job as a counsellor at a juvenile hall facility that lasted only a couple weeks then I got a job as a shoe salesman. That was more my speed… working with the public. I was always good with people. I had already proved that to myself as when I worked at the Hamburger Hamlet in Hollywood at the tender age of 18.

My father had been the main chef at the Sunset Strip Hamburger Hamlet Restaurant. It was the famous haunt of movie stars like Sinatra, Tony Curtis, Sammy Davis, Dean Martin, Rita Moreno, Lee Marvin, Anne Francis, Zsa Zsa Gabor and Bob Newhart. They all loved my dad. As one of the first chef's, at the original Hamburger Hamlet on the Sunset Strip, many of the stars of the day, would cook their burgers with dad. Throughout the years the Hamburger

Hamlet would see the likes of George Lucas and Angelina Jolie as loyal customers.

Apparently I got offered a part in the *Lone Ranger* television series when I was a baby. But Dad said he did not want his son to be an actor. Maybe seeing the reality of actors lives in Hollywood had something to do with his decision. I do remember seeing a picture of me & Silver the Lone Ranger's trusted steed..

However now that I have lived for over 33 years in London and worked as an actor in London's West End Theatres, its obvious my dad didn't get his wish after all. My father Bill Dortch had a serious work ethic. He worked 12 hours a day over a hot grill. He died in 1962.

When I was 18 years old I got a summer job at the Westwood *Hamburger Hamlet* in 1968. There was a camp West Indian fellow that worked on the, to go bar, I think his name was Horace. He was very popular but not nice to me so I was transferred to the original Sunset HH where my dad had worked.

I think it is an important legacy that Harry and Marylyn Lewis owners of the *Hamburger Hamlet* hired many African Americans… as these jobs, although hard work, were sought after and well paid. Dad's house was a huge two-story affair built in a semi Victorian style. It backed on to a mansion on the next street, which was owned by singer/bandleader Johnny Otis of 'Hand Jive' fame.

I remember seeing Otis's chauffer always washing the Rolls Royce in the driveway. I got to see the man himself in action when Johnny Otis gave my father tickets for us to see him support Sam Cooke in concert. I will never forget that experience…it was an indelible imprint on my consciousness for life

Ok I digress; back to Anchorage, Alaska. After working in the shoe store for a month I finally got my fare back to California and not a moment too soon as the freezing winter had well and truly arrived. Not even the sight of the beautiful aurora borealis with its amazing cascade of coloured lights often seen in the night sky above Anchorage could keep me there. I had to get home to Los Angeles.

Since I missed my window to go back to University in Riverside I decided to join Sedrick who had set up digs and started making contacts in LA. One of the first people he met was Spartacus R, the legendary bass player with *Osibisa*.

He was a hero of mine and our paths were destined to cross again over the years. There were so many scenes in LA… the Crenshaw District had clubs like *Mavericks Flat* and the *Total Experience* where a lot of top funk and soul bands would play.

Echo Park, a mainly Mexican area, had the Latin clubs, which would feature artists like Eddie Palmieri and Tito Puente. Sunset Strip in Hollywood had the *Whisky a Go Go, The Roxy, The Starwood* and the *Troubadour* where stars of the scene would ply their trade.

Out North Hollywood way there were Jazz clubs like the *Baked Potato* and local rock clubs for the wealthy youths of San Fernando Valley. Then there were places like Venice Beach, Santa Monica and Malibu where a lot of stars and Hollywood types lived.

One crowd Sedrick fell into was with P.P Arnold and Fuzzy Samuels. Pat "P.P" Arnold was famous in Europe. She had been an original *Ikettes* singer who was given a record deal in England. Mick Jagger produced a couple mega hits for Pat's debut album, which included 'The first cut is the deepest'.

Fuzzy Samuels played bass with *Crosby, Stills and Nash, Steven Stills and Manassas* and Linda Ronstadt. However he had been a session musician in London. Fuzz and Pat were married and had kids. They pretty much had an open house to us young aspiring musicians and always had some awesome jam sessions.

Pat & Fuzzy were renting one of Bob Dylan's houses in Malibu near Point Dume and it was no telling who you would meet at the house. One musician that used to hang there was Marlo Henderson who made his name playing guitar on Minnie Riperton records, another musician I remember was Hank Redd who played sax and guitar…he would go on to lead Stevie Wonder's band for many years.

I remember meeting DJ Rodgers who was a producer artist with a wealth of talent. He was always inviting musicians for a jam in the recording studio. What we didn't realise was that if anyone came up with a hook line or chorus that found its way on a hit record we had no recourse… because you rarely got copies of the recordings made at these jam sessions.

But for me being around these cats jamming; observing and listening to them was good schooling to learn about the music business. Networking with all these amazing musicians was nice but that did not put food on the table or earn us the valuable experience we needed as fledgling musicians.

I took a temporary job teaching kids reading and math at a school in East LA. The students were great and loved the fact that I was a musician. And apart from the odd sound of gunfire I loved my time there. Then Sedrick and I started rehearsing with a singing group called *Nature's Love.*

The guys who owned the rehearsal studio took Sedrick and I under their wings. We became like staff session musicians. We started doing gigs with a drummer we called Mighty Mighty! He had a foot that would not quit and played the bass drum with a double kick, which was great for funk bass lines.

We backed *Nature's Love* and other singers playing the local chitlin circuit clubs like the 'Name of the Game'. All we had to do was practice and study to keep our position as a tight rhythm section. It was also great to meet and jam with musicians who were on the session scene as they happily shared their knowledge of music.

I had loads of energy, a little knowledge and a half decent ear for music. I was pretty good at figuring out chord changes and bass lines, which was good, as most singers didn't have a clue.

One contact we made was a drummer named John Giddon he worked for HB Barnum a well known, music producer and arranger. We used to rehearse in Barnum's office after business hours if HB wasn't busy working on big band arrangements for Sammy Davis Jr.

Things were going really well, our backers in the Crenshaw district of LA had just given me money to buy a Fender bass and the showcases we were doing with *Nature's Love* received rave reviews among club owners and promoters. They were great singers with some, well rehearsed, dance moves that synced with the band's music. Their manager was a bit of a show off and always flashed a gun, which made me extremely uncomfortable.

Gun culture in America makes people do some crazy shit. I don't understand it. I'm afraid of guns and I was on a rifle team…I was a marksman. But when I did have a gun in the house purely for protection I used to hide it so far under my bed I would have struggled to get it in case of an emergency. Besides I was always told that if you carry a gun you don't flash it… or let anyone know you have a weapon.

Its common sense really. But most Americans are still playing cowboys and Indians in their adult life except the bullets are real. They refuse to acknowledge the danger in just keeping a weapon in the home until… its too late. Giving any old fool the power of God…to take a life, is just plain ignorant and barbaric.

Nature's Love was starting to get noticed by the *Total Experience* management who owned a club on Crenshaw Avenue. The men who ran the club were hustlers and amassed a little empire. Rumours about how they got their seed money ranged from insurance fraud to prostitution. But this was just speculation.

They owned a penthouse club on Sunset Strip called *Disco 9000*, a recording studio and a record label. Lonnie Simmons was the driving force behind the business and Total Experience Records launched the careers of two major acts *The Gap Band* with Charlie Wilson & *Yarborough and Peebles*.

But things were looking up for the singing group. There were deals on the table from *Total Experience* and *Mavericks Flat* who were both rivals. The band was poised for a massive breakthrough and then… disaster struck! The manager of *Nature's Love* was shot and killed by a jealous boyfriend of one of his girls and Leo a singer from the group shot the guy who murdered his manager.

It was a mess and everyone was shocked! Our backers pulled out and the gigs vanished. One of the singers got signed by *Total Experience Records*. So that was it then… no income! I moved back home to mums and started doing some gigs with Delmus Johnson backed by the old *Shango* band I had formed with Woody Diaz, Steve Campbell and Tony Campbell.

After a while I met this amazing lady named Yolanda, a sister of my friend Hope Luna. Yolanda wanted to move to LA and work at some massage parlour, all I had to do was go with her and she would look after me.

By that time Sedrick had met a guy named Gil Bottiglieri a New York Italian who had recorded and played with a band called *Little Sister,* an offshoot of *Sly and the Family Stone.* Gil was great… he played drums and clavinet and had a rehearsal space in the garage behind his house in the valley.

We had some great jam sessions and talked about putting a band together. He was also good for contacts, as he knew a lot of people in high places. I personally loved the New York accent Gil had, and he kept pigeons!!

Things were looking good again in LA and if there were gigs with Delmus in San Bernardino or Riverside I could still make the gig being only 45 miles away. Yolanda would go to work and I would be out gigging or jamming. She was a beautiful Mexican girl not one for marriage but very sexy. I started getting a bit too comfortable living as a kept man.

I knew it wasn't going to last long between Yolanda and me as she was looking after me but… it ended sooner than I thought. One day she came in and said she was going back to Riverside, that same day we got evicted from our apartment.

I wasn't too upset about our break-up Yolanda had shown me a lot of love and a huge amount of support for my music. Her sister Hope was gay and had actually spent a night a night with me, back in the day. It was the first time I had slept with a lesbian…what a revelation!! When it came to love making her sensuality was off the chain! Every molecule of my being was driven to new heights of sexual sustenance. It was an experience etched in the very core of my memory bank.

So when it came to her sister Yolanda entering into a temporary situation with me as her backup come lover I was extremely blessed to have this independent woman in my life.

It was a transitional time in my journey as a musician I knew good things were coming but they had better come quick.

A month before I had worked as a front of house usher for the Eartha Kitt musical 'Bread, Beans and Things'. It was being performed at the infamous Aquarius Theatre on the Sunset Strip where another ground breaking musical 'Hair' had premiered a few years earlier. After a short run of a week Miss Kitt decided to give a party at her home for the cast and crew. She came across as a very humbled extremely talented artist, this despite her being blacklisted for years in America after confronting the first lady Ladybird Johnson about the war in Vietnam. She said in no uncertain terms that our boys should be brought home from that inhumane war.

Her Beverley Hills home was converted horse stables, which once belonged to oil baron Edward Doheny who owned a huge area of Beverly Hills and its surrounding area.

It was a beautiful house in a little canyon off Sunset Boulevard complete with swimming pool and a little cabin at the top of the canyon, which she used as a creative space. She was an amazing host with a vast knowledge of politics and history.

Now after Yolanda left and I was made homeless I had to resign myself to my fate. I knew something was just around the corner for me. I had put in a lot of work developing my craft as a bass player. I had focused my youthful energy on the art of musical performance. It was a Zen thing. I met a tarot card reader in the Crenshaw district of LA a couple months earlier who, upon laying the cards out on the table said that my love life would have to take a back seat to my career plans. At the end of the line of cards was the sun card, which according to her was an omen that something huge was about to happen in my life.

I spent the first night sleeping in my car with everything I owned… a few clothes and my fender bass. I didn't even have guitar case. The next night I stayed with a piano player friend who lived in the valley. We went over to Gil's house for a jam. I just wanted to play the blues… God knows I had them.

Losing your girl and your flat on the same day, I guess I had hit rock bottom. Then Gil got a phone from someone looking for a bass player! There's an old saying that goes 'It's ok to hit rock bottom because when you hit the bottom there's only one way to go…and that's up.

The guy they were looking for wasn't there but I was, bass in hand, and ready to play. Someone came and bundled me in a station wagon and drove me just North of Santa Barbara to a ranch nestled between Solvang and Buellton. I wasn't told whom the gig was for until we were almost there. Finally the roadie said Joe Cocker was putting together a new band!

Chapter 3
LA Rock!

When I got there the vibe was weird! Henry McCullough of *Wings* fame was leaving and guitarist Albert Lee had arrived as his replacement along with Pete Gavin and Mick Weaver. Albert was an amazing cerebral player. Mick was an efficient keyboardist and Pete held the meter down. They were into everything from classic rock to country rock & jazz. I was deep into the funk but I had fit into their groove with my limited experience.

During our fist rehearsal they saw that I could hold down the rhythm down... even with my inexperience...and besides, Joe liked me. I had to quickly learn the material... luckily I owned a couple of Joe Cocker albums so I knew some of the tunes anyway.

I was clearly a novice with a very basic knowledge of music and these guys were heavyweights. However I could play the hell out of some funk... something they could not remotely understand in their wildest dreams.

We didn't have long before the first gig. Mick knew Joe's set having been a *Grease Band* member and Albert could play anything at anytime with anybody. So it was down to me, and the drummer Pete to form a solid rhythm section for the band.

Joe's new album 'I Can Stand a little Rain' had just been released with the lead track 'You are so beautiful' getting massive radio play. Joe was in his drinking stage at that time. Pete and Mick partied a bit but Albert was always in his room practicing 24/7. It was crazy... I just immersed myself into the music rehearsals which started sounding good. When the cocaine came out during one practice session I tried it... but couldn't function... so I left that shit alone!

The band lived on a ranch overlooking a very idyllic part of southern California... complete with fields of colourful flowers and on a good day a view of the Pacific Ocean. I got my first taste of traditional English cooking; steak and kidney pie, Yorkshire pudding and shepherd's pie.

The way the English rolled their joints was strange to me; they put in tobacco and mixed it with hash. I tried it once and it made me sick so I left that alone. Both Joe Cocker and Albert Lee met their future wives at that ranch and to give them credit…they are still together after all these years. Joe and Pam who were my roommates believe it or not were together until his death just as this book went to press, and Albert is still married to Karen.

It was important for me to maintain my side of keeping the music together as a bass player. No one was there to help, but somehow I had the most sought after gig in the business. Some of the guys wondered why someone as inexperienced as me should be in the band.

I'm sure they had friends they wanted in the band. But Joe liked me - we were roommates - he even took me shopping to get some clothes and stage outfits. Joe recognised me as a funk bass player and he loved it!

Finally we were ready to hit the road. We stayed at the Sunset Hyatt House Hotel on the strip. I even managed to get a lady friend to see me off and after rooming with Joe and *his* lady it was nice for me to spend some time with a young lady.

Reg Locke was the Tour Manager and the deal was that the band would split the profits equally with Joe Cocker 20% each gig. Considering he was getting around 50k average a gig with no more than 10k overheads it should have been around 8k a gig per man.

The cities we played:

Joe Cocker & The Cock n Bull Band Fall Tour 1974

Civic Arena Pittsburgh 9/23
Spectrum Philadelphia 9/28
Syracuse War museum 9/29
Duke University Durham NC 9/26
Lake Charles, Louisiana
Lafayette' Louisiana
Memphis, Tenn.
Atlanta, Georgia
Santa Ana, Texas
Dayton, Ohio
Akron, Ohio
Charlotte, SC

The initial tour started out really good, but I noticed Joe running to the back of the stage. Well it turns out he was throwing up; too much grog I suppose. This started happening more frequently - maybe it was nerves and alcohol. Shame, because the band were amazing and the material was great 'You are so beautiful' the single from the album had charted.

Rock and Roll and UFOs

It was the one song I used a chord chart for as they threw it in at the last moment. The rest of the songs had some nice grooves; anyway I like to think I made it all sound a little more, funky. Having only played as a semi-pro, I liked the feel of the big stage. I remember we played a gig in Austen, Texas where the bill was *Bad Company* with Jimmy Page, Joe Cocker, *Santana* and *ZZ Top*!

I had never heard of *ZZ Top* but they were head lining this festival with a 100,000 people in attendance! The roadies called it a tits and beer fest. Adapting to this new lifestyle was challenging and my internal mantra was: play music and make money. I resigned to keep myself to myself on tour so I didn't get into any kind of bad situations. I hung out with just two girls on the whole tour.

The plane journeys were starting to get to me. I was really nervous about flying and we were getting flights every other day. After playing twelve dates we took some rest and recuperation time in New Orleans. I had to let off some steam...

I went to a club and sat in with some guys from *Edgar Winter's White Trash*. Those guys could play some serious funk; they were really generous as well, with a nice energy. I got a little too tipsy At this point Joe Cocker and the band walked in. The guys on stage invited them up to play but they declined. At this point I said on the microphone what a bunch of cunts they were. Big mistake - I got fired the next day.

Reg Locke gave me two thousand dollars and said Joe would give me my share of the money when they got back to LA. Well, I never got paid, In retrospect I should have gotten something written on paper although a verbal agreement is as good as a written one in this case and there were witnesses.

I met Reg Locke 12 years later at Ronnie Woods house in London; he bragged to Ronnie how he discovered me. Not mentioning the fact that Joe Cocker still owed me at least sixty thousand dollars.

I encountered some really good people whilst on tour ... one guy was Conrad Isidore who had played drums on Joe Cockers famous *Mad Dogs and Englishmen* Tour. He was a West Indian musician who grew up in London but he still had his West Indian rhythms and sensibility.

This included a cultural flow that would encompass the culinary delights of his native Aruba. As you tasted the spices in the soup and hit the smooth rhythmic patterns drilled into the repetitive sway of the island melodies... the awareness of entering a new world dawned on my present being.

I learned a lot from Conrad. My best mate Sedrick Jackson and I used to go to his house and jam until 4 or 5am. Conrad worked on the session scene in London and his reputation was getting international attention. For many years Conrad and Fuzzy Samuels were the rhythm section for Eddie Grant and played on many of the *Equals* recordings as well as with Stephen Stills' *Manassas* and Robert Palmer's *Vinegar Joe*.

I met drummer Reggie Isidore through Conrad - he was Conrad's younger sibling. Reggie had just been fired from Robin Trower's band after playing on his two million selling albums including the classic 'Bridge of Sighs'. But Reggie was a well known hothead and I am proud to say we would be good friends for many years.

Reggie and I used to jam all the time playing funk and rock riffs. One night after a jam with Joe Jammer (*Olympic Runners*) we were invited to dinner, by a guy named Hank. The restaurant was amazing it was in Hollywood it looked like a mosque, you sat at low tables on the floor and were served a middle-eastern type cuisine.

The place was filled with celebrities and stars. One of the guests at our tables was Mike Vernon famous British producer and owner of Blue Horizon Records. And yes he produced some recordings that my friend Gregg Schaeffer played on.

Reg told him that I was a great bass player and had just done Joe Cocker's tour. He said Eric Burdon was looking for a bass player and that he would recommend me. Mike gave me the telephone number to Far Out Productions. I called them and arranged to have a play with the band which was Aalon Butler on guitar and Alvin Taylor on drums.

Everything went well during that first blow I knew a lot of the songs already having listened to Eric Burdon's new album album Sun Secrets. Terry McVey was the tour manager, Jerry Goldstein produced the album and Steve Gold was the manager of the whole operations.

Far Out Productions looked after *War*, Robben Ford, Jimmy Witherspoon and *The Booty People*. They had a rehearsal studio on sight so everything was in house with offices and a recording studio. I pretty much had the gig the only snag was they were still auditioning bass players.

I remember Spartacus coming by to audition…he was my hero having played with *Osibisa* and it was my pleasure to listen to him play with the band but he didn't get the gig. But one day I got to rehearsal and Tim Bogart turned up - oh my God the same bassist who had just made an album with Jeff Beck and Carmine Appice!

They were called *Beck Bogart and Appice*. It was a super band as Bogart and Appice had played with *Vanilla Fudge* and Jeff Beck was just the great Jeff Beck. As he strapped on his bass Tim gave me sly grin then he started playing with the band. I had just smoked a little ting with Aalon so I was buzzing but still not prepared for his kick ass bass playing skills.

Bogart was like Jimi Hendrix on that bass and I was like…there goes my gig. They were really into it. I just packed up my bass and left. Properly humiliated I went back home and practiced. Sometimes its not just your playing abilities that get you work… most times it's a combination of skill and personality.

I knew I was a steady bassist and I could definitely hold down a groove so I would get work very soon. As I was mentally building my confidence, playing my bass, I was starting to feel better. Then the phone rang it was the office, Far Out's office; they wanted to know why I left rehearsal as I was still on the payroll!

I came back to rehearsals and Aalon had a cheeky grin on his face. He said that joint must have tripped me out. I said if Jimi Hendrix turned up for your job you would have done the same thing. Anyway rehearsals continued with no more auditions. John 'Rabbit' Bundrick who would go on and play with *The Who* for many years joined us on piano and Hammond organ. Rabbit was another popular session player based in London; he had played keyboards in Johnny Nash's band *Sons of the Jungle* with Bob Marley. He was from Lubbock, Texas and had some great stories about being on the road with Bob.

We played a lot of dates… I think the tour lasted over 6 months. We would headline large club dates and would support artists like *Grand Funk Railroad* and *Lynyrd Skynyrd* in the arenas and concert halls. We got so tight we were blowing these bands away every night!

I remember playing a date in Detroit we were on the bill with a band called *Camel* where I met Pete Bardens the keyboard player. Pete was a really nice humble guy and we would meet again in London years later and become very good friends. Although the band toured all over America some of the dates were at venues I had previously played with Joe Cocker a couple months earlier.

People would say weren't you just here with Joe Cocker and I would say that would be me. When we played in Atlanta, Georgia at the Omni supporting *Grand Funk*…we were invited to the Playboy Club for a jam as our stable mates Jimmy Witherspoon was playing there. That was great! Reg Isidore was playing drums in Jimmy's band. It was a very special session… we were on fire; so much so that when *Grand Funk* showed up they wouldn't play.

We left with a bevy of Playboy Bunnies…Naima and Loretta were local Atlanta girls and were the first black playboy bunnies I had ever met. Naima would later join me on some dates and would eventually move to California. Loretta would go on to work with film producer, director and actor Tyler Perry

We did a Southern tour with *Grand Funk Railroad* that took us to my hometown of Memphis where I finally got to spend some time with a lady named Bessie Mae. I had a crush on her since I was seven years old. This was better than getting together with a groupie because I knew her and it just made me feel better.

We got a chance to meet the most famous groupie in America. Her name was Sweet Connie and *Grand Funk Railroad* mentions her in their seminal hit 'We're an American Band'. Connie walked into Eric Burdon's hotel room while we were having a meeting and declared 'Which one of you is Eric Burdon? I been wanting to suck his cock since I was ten years old'.

At this point all the black guys in the band including me put our hands up and said I'm Eric Burdon. It was quite a funny episode but Eric seemed to enjoy his time with this sexual icon.

Eric had some awesome stories of life on the road; he took it all in his stride.

When I toured with Joe Cocker I kept the groupie thing in check, as it was my first tour and I had to keep my head together. But now this was my second tour and we were out for a long time and I was single.

Now I wasn't exactly a new man and advances of feminism were prevalent in the white, black and Latino communities. I had heard of Erica Jong's book 'Fear of Flying' on female sexuality. However having been taught about sex when I was a 12 year old by the babysitter who was a busty girl of 19 named Jimmy Lee was extremely helpful. Although I appreciated the sensual aspects of love making, I did have problems stripping away the aspects of male chauvinism from my consciousness. I guess its like racism... ingrained into very fabric of ones being.

I did appreciate the independence of women after all, my mother, had been both independent and a feminist. She always owned her house so if a man got out of line he had to hit the door. She was also an astute businesswoman, something I was to learn more about after her death. I knew not to ever force myself on woman besides after introductions if a lady was interested... you would know soon enough. So when we had groupies throwing themselves at us it was a strange dilemma.

It got so bad that at times I just wanted to meet a woman, any woman not connected to the music scene in anyway. Most times I just rolled with the groupie thing but the best times I had were with ladies I would meet away from the venues. I just felt they liked me for who I was... not what band I played in. This was very important to me as a man I suppose. I guess I'm lucky that most women I've met have always trusted me, this has put me into some interesting situations.

Flash forward to London in the early 1990's I happened to spend the night with a well known journalist, she lived in a very expensive flat in Notting Hill, West London. I must have been at the height of my sensual aggrandizement as my proclivities toward matters of a sexual nature were that of a very tender lover. After our romantic session the lady held me tight then looked me in the eye and said she had been a victim of the Notting Hill rapist and I was the first person she made love to since that terrible episode in her life and she thanked me. I just held her and cried.

The Eric Burdon Band was billed as an act from England however Eric was the only English person in a band that boasted three African Americans and two Texans as Snuffy Waldon had now joined us on lead guitar.

Snuffy Waldon was an awesome guitarist, he had played with a tight three piece band from Texas called *Stray Dog* and would go on to play with Chaka Khan and become a very successful TV and film composer.

I had seen *Stray Dog* live at the *Whiskey a Go Go* and knew them from a rehearsal studio I used to work and hangout at. Nashville. Snuffy went on to compose many TV scores including *Ally Mcbeal* and *The Wonder Years*.

The girls on tour loved us and I had a knack of getting in there with the ladies, don't know why though. I was of average height and you could hardly call me drop dead gorgeous. We came to spend some time in Gainesville, Florida - a college town, *full* of women!

The girls literally setup camp at our hotel; it was embarrassing - it was like they were standing in line taking turns. I generally have a need to think somebody likes me for myself and not because I played in a band. Yes… I'm pretty naïve.

I was invited to a strip club one night. When I got there I met the owner's daughter and ended up taking her back to my hotel along with five strippers. I called Rabbit and said the party got started in my room. Well Rabbit in his excitement, forgot to lock the door to his room and later discovered someone had taken his bag which about $1,500.00 cash in it.

Rabbit seemed to be far more worried about his cassette tapes of original compositions that were in the bag, than the money. However the next day Danny Sims, who published Rabbit and Bob Marley, sent him a cheque for $1,500.00. This was one of two orgies I remember having with Rabbit in that town. Someone said the woman out numbered the men in Gainesville ten to one.

One night after our gig there I was smoking a doobie with two male fans. There was a knock on the door and when I opened it this beautiful lady came in and asked the two guys to leave. She told me she was married, had never cheated on her husband but she just had to have me. It was one of the most magical nights I ever spent with someone.

Since most of the groupies were Anglo, I thought I was doing something amazing for race relations in America…well if only. My other Playboy Club experience would be in Chicago where we had played another steaming gig in a club except this time I was the only one who pulled and this girl was an amazing looking blond and everybody was jealous.

We went to see Flo & Eddie from the *Turtles* and Frank Zappa's band. Well afterwards we all went to *Denny's* with Flo & Eddie. I sat apart from the musicians with my playboy bunny and someone decided to have a massive food fight rock n roll style. It was insane but I saw my chance to get away from guys and go back to the hotel with the young lady so we could chill.

By the time the tour started heading towards New York the clubs and concerts along the Eastern Seaboard things were starting to get weird. At one of these gigs someone slipped us something called MDA or was it STP? Anyway I was never into the heavy stuff really.

This drug was like a combination of psychedelics and speed…at one point we had to hold hands… Eric Burdon was telling us that this band would go on to great heights and it was the band he had waited for all these years. He said Jimi Hendrix had missed his chance to play in a band with Eric.

From that time the Hendrix vibe got heavier and heavier... I remember Eric had one of Hendrix's guitars at his house in Palm Desert, California, I remember it was a Gibson Les Paul with a sunburst colour and very beautiful.

One of the clubs we played in just before we hit New York had a Jimi Hendrix copy band supporting us. The singer/guitarist looked just like Hendrix!! It was spooky because Hendrix had been dead for almost two years. The world was still recovering from his death.

Flying into New York during the daytime is breath taking... the cityscape just jumps out at you very dramatically. We played several dates at the famous Bottom Line Club. It was a great vibe and on our last night legendary British bluesman John Mayall joined us on stage.

We had an amazing jam session... they literally had to drag John off the stage. After the gig we had guests from an off Broadway show about Jimi Hendrix called 'The Electric Warrior'. The shows producer and lead actor came in. The actor was the spitting image of Hendrix. The producer said he wanted Eric to play the part of Jimi's manager.

This was the final straw for Eric he was definitely spooked[*]. Eric took a flight immediately back to LA after the gig. I don't know why, but it felt like, he was being haunted, by Jimmy Hendrix. Well the band had a few days R n R left in New York and we were going to enjoy it.

I met a lady at our last show in New York who, would be in my life for a few years her name was Ingrid. A very exotic looking woman with a German accent, she was from Nuremburg; her mother was German and her dad was an African American from the US. She had dated Lester Chambers from the *Chamber Brothers* but she was single, and I could not believe my luck.

We became very close during my stay in New York, when I left for LA we vowed our eternal love and she would join me soon on the West Coast. We had one more leg of the tour to do in California we did the club circuit from Santa Barbara to Redwood City and played San Francisco where I met an old friend named Rob Lopes. He was a young guitarist I met through Gregg Schaeffer back in the day.

Our Last gig was to be five nights at the Roxy Theatre in Hollywood. It was recorded and filmed every night. This was the climax of a long tour and the audience loved every minute of it. Jimmy Witherspoon was our support band so I got to hang with my mate Reg Isidore who was still drumming for Jimmy. 'Eric Burdon Live at the Roxy' would be released later when I lived in England.

A strange thing happened after the gig. Alvin Taylor came up to me and asked me had I checked with the musicians union because there may be some cash for me there.

---

[*] Possibly because Hendrix's manager had been Chas Chandler, an original member of *The Animals* along with Eric Burdon. JD

I didn't realise that because they were recording the band there were session fees due beyond our normal gig salary. I went to the Local 47 Musicians Union and enquired about the session fee and they handed me a cheque for over three thousand dollars!

I thought it was good of Alvin to tell me about this because nobody else did and it probably would still be there. That added to a nice little packet for over six months of touring. And to cap it all off the waitress from the Roxy came home with me for a night of unbridled passion!! My adventure for the time being was at an end and it was time to make plans for my new career in the music business.

Chapter 4
Something in the Desert Sky

Woody Diaz and Jeannie Hostetler had moved to Echo Park in LA, not far from my digs in Hollywood. Woody came to me with a proposition to put the *Shango* band back together. He had access to an empty house on Bunker Hill over looking Chinatown and the LA skyline and a back garden that overlooked Dodger stadium!

The rent was fifty dollars a month as it was earmarked for demolition at some point in the future. It had loads of rooms and could accommodate up to four people with room for a rehearsal space. It was perfect.

Steve and Tony Campbell agreed to start the band again and move to LA. Steve, Tony and I moved into the house... we reformed the band with Woody, got a couple of agents and started gigging.

At first we called the band *Fire and Ice* then we chose the name *Spice*. The core band was a four piece fronted by Tony and myself. We had Gil Bottiglieri and Rick Bowles at various times on keyboards. We had three different sets of horn players to use depending on the budget for the gigs

We were really focused on our musicality and creativity. I got up in the morning early, everyday and practiced my bass for 2 hours. Then I would move over to guitar, which I used to write songs and dedicate 2 hours to writing.

In the afternoon I would make business calls and then we would all meet for band rehearsal. Then we would go out and do gigs, which would consist of playing between four and six forty-five minute sets. It was like being in boot camp for musicians. Mike Kenny from *Iron Maiden* joined us for six months before moving to England.

We started getting noticed fairly quickly by people in the industry... there were two guys named Bob and Fred who were connected with Motown. They heard some of our material and put us in the studio to record some demos. They brought in a horn section, Mike and John

Bolivar, who put the sweetening on our tracks.

Mike and John were like the *Brecker Brothers* except they both played sax. Bob and Fred also brought in another singer guitarist to compliment our rock funk sound; his name was Paul Sabu, and he was the son of the famous Indian actor Sabu.

We recorded a couple tracks with him and did some gigs together but in the end Sabu was headed for a different direction musically than us. He was into a more raw edge sound like metal. We on the other hand had the rock edge with a funk bottom and gospel harmonies.

We continued giving our songs to Bob and Fred until we were invited to record at Motown studios in the sunset room where Diana Ross did most of her recordings. Cal Harris was engineering, and we did one of my songs called Young Bird, it was similar to the type of song *Earth Wind and Fire* would someday do.

The feedback from Motown was that the band needed more work but they offered me a writing deal. This proposal put me into a difficult situation with the band and would cause rifts that would lead to our break up eventually. I was loyal to the guys though and turned the down the deal.

I then got offered a singles deal from Harvey Fuqua over at RCA as they wanted to use our voices on tracks that had already been recorded by session musicians. This did not appeal to Steve and Tony, as our playing would not be featured. But they could not see this as a steppingstone for promotion and radio play. So I turned down yet another deal.

Harvey Fuqua would go on to co-produce the 'Sexual Healing' album with Marvin Gaye. I ended up being blacklisted by Motown because one of my melodies ended up on a Marvin Gaye album and after we the band did not get a deal with Motown we decided to take them to court for copyright infringement of my song.

Cal Harris who had just recorded me at Motown was the engineer for the Marvin Gaye album. We had Motown dead to rights. Bob and Fred disappeared and stopped returning calls. Meanwhile our band Spice got offered a tour of Canada as a backing band for Diane Brookes who had an album out on Sinatra's Warner Reprise label.

Diane had worked on a lot of albums as a backing singer and was dating one of the famous Farragher Brothers who appeared on the album along side members of *The Band*, top LA session players James Gadson, Wah Wah Watson with Bonnie Raitt and Anne Murray on backing vocals. Brian Ahern produced the album so there was a good budget for us musicians.

We rehearsed at *The Carpenters* rehearsal studios and by the time we hit the Ottawa National Theatre we were so tight as a band… the critics declared 'Too much Spice for Diane Brooks' in the press. At a gig in Kitchner there was chicken wire strewn across the front of the stage Blues Brother's style with a lot of broken glass on the floor.

Were the audience throwing bottles at the previous band? We actually got an awesome reception by the locals and the support act was the award winning, music comedy duo, McClean and McClean. They were great and often took the piss out of us every night.

After the Canadian tour we started working with a singer named Wayne Anthony who sang with the *Rev James Cleveland's Choir*. Wayne would go on to appear in the *Blues Brothers* movie as a soloist with *Rev James Cleveland's Choir* and James Brown.

Wayne entered our band into a national battle of the bands contest organised by a national soul radio station with the winners supporting *Chaka Khan & Rufus* and *KC and the Sunshine Band*. Initially I was appalled as I looked at our band as being a professional unit however we were persuaded by Wayne to do it as we would get a lot of exposure.

So we decided to play a medley of 10 current hits by the likes of *The Jacksons* and *Earth Wind and Fire*. Dressed in the new stage gear, we had just bought from our tour of Toronto we were a site to behold. We were playing the Shrine auditorium in Los Angeles and when the curtains opened up on us every girl in the place sighed...we had won the contest before playing one note!

We blew all the bands away and came in second all around and first in the band division. The combination of Wayne's gospel voice with our harmonies and tight rhythm section was unbeatable.

One storming gig we had was backing Gene Redding (Otis Redding's cousin) at the Starwood Club in Hollywood. Norman Whitfield and Buddy Miles were amongst those in the audience. We were the perfect band for Gene Redding's raw edgy soulful tones. Gene was an electrifying performer, I had hired him as one of my supporting acts when I promoted the Elton John gig.

Alvin Taylor had played drums for Gene's band back in the day. I remembered this when we played together in Eric Burdon's band. Alvin would go on to record with the likes of Elton John, George Harrison, Leo Sayer and Gil Scott Heron.

Playing the Military bases was our bread and butter gigs... we must have played every military base in California. We stopped a race riot at Oceanside marine base once. It was a weird gig with black soldiers on one side of the room and white soldiers on the other side.

One white and one black soldier were about to start a fight. I told the band to crank up the volume and we played 'Smoke on the Water' which stunned the whole room into silence. Then we broke in down with a mellow *Earth Wind and Fire* song. We got a big applause!

I then told the soldiers that 'if you want to fight... go on... we'll pack up our gear and go home'. Both Black and White soldiers said 'no don't leave'. We played our set and brought peace to the club. Afterwards a white soldier came up to me and said ' a half hour ago he was about to throw a bottle of beer at my face but he said he liked what I did and asked if he could buy me a beer.

For a brief minute we brought the soldiers together through something as ambiguous as art. They temporarily forgot all the prejudices, traditions, axioms, loyalties and testimonies of our birthright that were programmed into our being long before we were born. Sometimes you forget the possibility of danger when you play a gig.

The miracle of music can have tragic consequences such as with the Stones in Altamount where the Hells Angels went berserk and killed a member of the audience. Thank the creator that these types of incidents are the exceptions rather than the norm.

It seemed the utopia we hippies and like-minded people dreamt about has become a superfluous blip that could be easily quashed by the onslaught of the coming new technology and the corporate entities setup to deliver such systems and ideals.

All conflict in the world is just a reflection of the conflict in our heads. How can we move forward when that march, is stilted by superstition, false doctrines, misconceived ambitions and obsolete standards. Perhaps in a future scenario man will free himself from the contamination of our irrational past. Where a new, enlightened state could arise and break the mould of draconian methods of thought.

There was a gig we had to do at an Air Force base near Joshua Tree. We drove from LA all the way to base only to find we were meant to play the next night. So on the way back home we pulled over in the desert for a beer and to smoke a small joint. We sat in the back of the van and starting talking.

I started getting all philosophical saying that world was becoming like an LCD chip board with transistors and capacitors sending out waves of energy. I said there were probably multi universes that could fit in the eye of a needle. Then in my minds eye I saw an image of Los Angeles from the air, which shrunk and morphed into the size of an LCD circuit board but smaller

Suddenly the conversation got really surreal and I notice I'm hearing voices but, nobody is talking. The guys, in the band, their eyes were like glass like... they were in a trance. Then a voice in my head said 'We are here, do you want to come with us?'.

I suddenly felt scared and withdrew into myself... I didn't know what was going on.

Then gravity started weighing on my bladder, the beer had to come out. We all got up like robots filed out of the van and started peeing in the desert. I looked up at the stars and saw two white lights flying in geometrical patterns. This was so bizarre no one said anything about it and we didn't get back to LA until 3am!

Somehow, a twenty-minute stop turned in three or four hours we could not account for. Well Woody and I dropped off Gil in the Valley and I think as we were turning into Sherman Oaks

Boulevard we saw two policemen pointing at the sky and lo and behold there was a low flying craft, saucer shaped with luminous tentacles cruising the night sky in North Hollywood.

I yelled at the police 'you see it we see it'. The next day in the *LA Times* it reported that UFO's buzzed Desert towns. I called the Times and said I was out in the desert that night something did happen. They said they would get someone to follow up my story but they never did.

The really strange thing was that no one in the band talked about it. It was like the memory had been taken from them. Woody said he knows something happened but wasn't sure. Three UFO related incidents in one night… very strange never happened again though.

The next night we did the gig at the air-force base. I sang 'Always and Forever' and I hit some tones that were almost supernatural. The girls in clubs were transfixed on the PA speaker from which my voice was coming. I guess I sang as if my life depended on it like the phrase… 'Hope to die'.

As an artist sometimes you experience oneness with the universe like a synchronicity with all that exists. I have had these revelations on quite a few occasions due to the nature of my career and I'm sure many other artists have had the same. My UFO encounter or what ever had a definite effect on me. Exactly what type of effect this experience would have on me only time would tell.

We got booked to play a rock venue in the Valley in North Hollywood, this place had Hells Angels as customers. These guys were not known to like black people but they *loved* our band and we played the club for several months. We had the right balance of rock and soul that served us well in the late seventies post hippie period.

Our band Spice was building a great reputation as backing musicians for solo artists. Our next project was as backing band for Lee Garrett. Lee was a blind singer songwriter who had penned hits 'Sign Sealed Delivered', 'Lets Get serious' (Jermaine Jackson) 'It's a Shame' (*The Spinners*) with Stevie Wonder.

The objective was to provide musical support for Lee on a couple of shows with the idea of going on a national tour. We had a jam with Lee and got on very well, this was before his collaboration with Jermaine Jackson and Stevie Wonder on the 'Lets Get Serious Hit'.

We were to be paid for two weeks rehearsals then do shows, which would be attended by top booking agents. Everything was going well with rehearsals Lee was a dynamic performer who was signed to Chrysalis Records and had a minor R&B hit with, 'You're my every**thing'** from his solo album 'Heat for the Feet'.

During the second week Lee had run out of money but he had paid for the first weeks rehearsals. Steve and Tony decided not to do the gig but Woody and I argued that we had put in time for rehearsals and the gigs were booked and we should see it through.

The brothers Campbell were not having it so I had to tell Lee that the band would not be backing him on his gigs. I told him that Woody and I really wanted to do it but Steve and Tony were adamant that they would not be on board. Lee was devastated... so was I really. You see sometimes it's not just about the money, I mean you have to have good business skills to survive in this business.

But often you have to make judgements calls above the immediate future. I mean we invested time in Lee's project and got half the money and as gigs were booked we could have worked something out with Lee and supported him so he could get through the gigs.

I didn't realise it at the time but Lee had been getting ripped off, of his publishing royalty cheques, by a girlfriend. About a couple weeks later I turned on the TV and there was Lee Garrett on a balcony with a shotgun to his head.

He had had enough and wanted to end it all. It was only Stevie Wonder who talked him out of committing suicide. This was all over the news. I felt like shit and the actions of Steve and Tony spelt the end of the band for me.

We had to give up the house on Bunker Hill as the demolition date was near. I missed that place... I could see the LA cityscape from my bed; a scene that inspired me over the years to practice my music, song writing and performance skills. There was a small Spanish castle type house next door and the guy who lived there gave some awesome parties, he was gay but he knew some beautiful ladies.

There was always a movie or a commercial being filmed on Bunker Hill or at my gay neighbour's house including 'Ironside' with Raymond Burr, and 'Mother Jugs and Speed' starring Harvey Keitel, Raquel Welch and Bill Cosby.

We moved to a nice modern place Steve and Tony found in the exclusive Silverlake district. The band dynamic changed... the brothers started trying to lord it over me. We continued doing gigs until Steve and I got into a fight.

I forgot what it was all about except that during one of our gigs I had met a beautiful mixed race girl whose father was African American and her mother Japanese. She was beautiful and she wanted to sleep with me... she was a virgin and she chose me for her first time so we had a very special night together. In terms of relationships, I had too many women in my life at the time so I introduced her to Steve.

Steve would end up marrying her and they had two kids. At the time we had the fight I don't really know where he was coming from. Maybe Steve was just pissed off at me or jealous. Anyway I moved out and moved into a studio apartment. I decided I would go to London as I still had an open invitation from Reg Isidore.

There was a lovely lady who lived next door who was a bit of a female shaman she was Anglo with some kind mix as she had black curly hair. She said she was a white witch as she clutched her Egyptian Book of the Dead. However I found her sexuality alluring maybe I fell under her spell. She swore that I was a re-born Nubian prince and gave me an Egyptian robe, which I in turn gave to my mother. I always felt an affinity to Egypt and would…years later read a profound book 'Black Athena' by Martin Bernal on African Egypt and the legacy they left for civilization.

This book is a treatise on the European conspiracy in rewriting history and promoting racist, Europocentric historiography giving credit to the Greeks for knowledge that existed when they were a primitive, mountain dwelling tribes. This travesty was enforced by, the British, Spanish and Germans at different times in history to promote the Aryan Model through history and religion. It was all about justifying African slavery and dehumanizing millions of people through the use of the slave code which robed people of their language religion and culture thus re-branding them as little more than animals.

Yes the whole thing about classical Greek knowledge was a fabrication. Egypt had colonies in Greece and taught them math, philosophy and sciences. All a part of a European plan to subjugate whole nations of Afroasiatic people and indeed as much of the world as possible… see the British Empire. Every war on this planet has served to promote the hubris of those Europeans who would force their world order on us all. Just read the book… the author is a European who graduated from Cambridge, taught government studies at Cornell University and tells the truth.

Until the destructive lies are revealed and the contributions of African people are credited, the world will stay in a state of flux with no religious, social or cultural truth. We all of us whether African, Asian or European deserve to know the real story of our roots. They say knowledge is power. Is that why the powers that be keep us steeped in religious social conflict and ignorance? The truth would diminish their hold on the masses and the balance of power would change. I personally believe we are being observed and as the despots in charge continue to promote war and destruction we are not only a danger to our immediate universe but others as well.

Besides the club gigs I had a part time job working as a wholesale florist who delivered flowers and floral supplies to flower shops. My route was Orange County and after finishing club gigs I'd go to the flower market for 3am.

After securing my flowers and flower products… then loading up the truck. My delivery cycle started from 8am to 12pm. Afterwards it was home to sleep then up again to play gigs then back to the flower market.

In time I managed to save over one thousand dollars cash plus money for my flight ticket to London. I gave up my apartment put my things in storage and said my goodbyes and was ready for my next adventure. You know fate can be a real bastard sometimes although I felt something was on the horizon for me.

I was going by bus to New York to get a flight to London…that was my plan. On the day I was to leave tragedy struck; I lost my tickets and almost a thousand dollars in cash. It must have fallen out of my pocket at the bus station.

All I can say is that I wish the person who found the money and the ticket needed it more that I did. But it was my fate. I stayed at my mums for a bit, then my brother Tony told me that Motown bassist James Jameson lived around the corner and that I should try to get some bass lessons from him.

We went around to his house and I could not believe it! There stood the man who played bass on most of the Motown hits that ever charted. Mr Jameson agreed to give me a few lessons but only on the upright bass.

I hadn't played bass violin properly since high school. But I did not want to miss this chance. He would meet me at the door with a whiskey in hand and set about showing me the basic techniques on playing the upright bass.

You'd never know that on many of the early Motown hits James Jameson played the upright bass. He was slapping the bass and playing octaves on hit's way before Larry Graham or Mark King. He had a degree in music, and was a great, sight-reader.

I had to get my life back together after my misfortune. I had a jam with this guitarist named Jonathon Markowitz he invited me to stay at his place. Through Jonathon I met the Malibu/Venice Beach musicians. Johns father was Richard Markowitz who was a music composer for TV and film among the many TV series he had written included *Wild Wild West* and *Murder She Wrote*.

John' sister Kate was also talented and was dating Michael Franks at the time. We went to a jam session one night at Alfred Johnson's house with members of *Little Feat* and a newly signed singer Rickie Lee Jones.

She would go on to have a hit with 'Chuck E's in Love'. Alfred Johnson had three co-writes on her debut album as well. Riki was cool... she seemed a bit shy, even though she was dating Tom Waits at the time. Alfred Johnson was amazing! He was this genus African American who was an engineer at Hughes Aircraft, played amazing piano and was a good songwriter. You would often see him play his piano on Venice Beach's promenade.

Apparently he still plays on the beach to this day. Jonathon's father hired me, John, his sister Kate Markowitz and another singer to do backing vocals on a film sound track called *The Boss's Son* starring Rita Moreno.

To our great surprise the singer that we would be backing was none other than Richie Havens! We were all star struck and he was such a gracious gentleman. However when he pulled out a little figure of ET the alien and said 'they are here and they will make their presence known soon' and gave me a knowing smile.

Did he know something? Havens had a shamanic aesthetic when he performed. Just check out Woodstock and see the prophetic nuance of his mystical apparition on stage. And in light of my recent UFO experience nothing surprised me.

I met a lovely girl from Chicago named Mary Polk she worked for the Nederlander Corporation… they produced musicals and plays and owned theatres all over America. We would go see musicals at the Pantages theatre in Hollywood as she would get free tickets.

We broke up after a couple months and I found myself homeless again. But I managed to get a part time job as assistant manager of an apartment building. This included accommodation, so I had a roof over my head.

It was during this time that I would meet my next girlfriend her name was Fumiko and was from Nakano, Japan. She spoke very little English so we got on really well and would be together for almost three years. My sister Stephanie told that a new project was looking for musicians and actors. This was a CETA backed project with government funding. The wages were not high but it afforded a chance to earn as you learn. I went for the interview… and got the job. It was a chance to be mentored and learn musical comedy theatre from the imitable Ernie Glucksman.

Ernie had been Jerry Lewis's manager and producer and a gag writer for Rowan and Martin's 'Laugh In'. Ernie had produced *The Nutty Professor* and *The Bellboy* films and he was to become a major influence in my life long after his death.

Ernie took me under his wing. I started off as the bass player in the orchestra then got promoted to comedy actor. Things were looking up for me again. The acting project was at the Young Israel Building on Fairfax near West LA.

It was a project, which consisted of retired Hollywood film and theatre actors and musicians. We put a musical together called *Go Like 60s* because most of the cast were over 60 years of age except for me and, a fellow actor.

The musical director of the project was Henry Tobias of the famous *Tobias Brothers* who had written hits since the 1930s. Sammy Wolf was one of the comedians he had been in the original Stooges vaudeville act, which later became the *3 Stooges*.

Babe Wallace, who starred in *Stormy Weather* with Lena Horne and Bill 'Bojangles' Robinson, joined the cast. We became good friends. Babe was the first African American to appear on Broadway, he had lived in France as a performer in *Le Folies Bergère* and lived and performed in Israel.

Babe was a great raconteur who could recall some amazing stories. He was a friend of Louis 'Satchmo' Armstrong and had been a conductor for *Cab Calloway's Orchestra*. While he was in LA he was staying at an apartment building owned by Mae West whom he had known from the old days. Babe was always writing songs.

He had written for Cab Calloway and before he died one of his songs, 'A Chicken Ain't Nothing but a Bird' was featured in a Burger King commercial in the Americas!

Young Israel was a centre of Jewish life in Los Angeles. They had some books and doctrines that were hundreds maybe thousands of years old. Whilst looking through one such book I happened across a passage that said black people were on this earth as direct voice to God. My cousin Reverend Elvesta Robertson always told me that the Africans they put into slavery and brought to the Americas were mostly Hebrews and Israelites!!! Now it seems that the proof through DNA evidence is there for all to see.

Not only are most African Americans descended from the Hebrews they have found pockets of tribes around Africa like the Lemba in Zimbabwae and the Falashas of Ethiopia that are the original Jews. However the Europeanisation of Israel is now complete with Ashkenazi Jews, whose roots are Eastern Europe, claiming to be Gods chosen people. This lie is perpetrated so the United States government will continue to have a presence in the Middle East for purposes of oil revenue and political currency.

Babe Wallace lived and worked in Israel, he seemed to know about our legacy as the lost tribe. His parting words to me were to learn Hebrew and French before I die. So in 2016 Muslim terrorist groups ISIL and Al Qaeda are destroying all historical evidence of an African presence in the Middle East. Keep in mind these terrorist groups got their seed money from the CIA. As the military industrial Complex tries in earnest to keep us in the dark on orders of the families that run this planet, scientists are discovering new technologies that contradict the lies we have been taught.

Apparently the Sphinx, thought originally to be 5,000 years, is at least 10,000 years old and some have claimed it could be over 50,000 years old. Now with the discovery of pyramids in the Crimea said to be made during the age of the dinosaurs it seems the real history of this planet is coming to the fore despite the massive cover ups which stem from the time of Emperor Constantine through to the Spanish Inquisition right on up until today.

It seems that a lot of European Jewish rabbis know about the legacy of African Americans and their claim to being the lost Hebrew tribe. But unfortunately the winds of change and truth do not blow through the halls of Capital Hill. As they continue to exert domination over the real children of God I wonder what thoughts are with those that watch us from afar. Any destruction on our planet would have ramifications in other universes millions of light years away.

I believe the Vatican and European Jews have a lot to answer for regarding the conflict the world is facing today. There are some things I felt Babe was afraid to tell me or maybe he thought I wasn't ready for the real knowledge. One thing for sure in the time of Moses and Ramesses those people were Black Africans not European as depicted in movies for a millennium. The Old Testament, was written by Black Africans, and the oldest Christian society on the planet earth is in Ethiopia. But for the time being I was happy to be working, keeping my head down and learning my craft at Young Israel.

I kept my contacts in the flower industry for occasional jobs like decorating Hugh Hefner's Playboy Mansion West for a new years party leading to 1979. What a layout, aesthetically pleasing in everyway as was the staff. We turned the foyer of that gothic mansion into a winter wonderland theme. From the contacts I made at the Playboy mansion I was invited to a film premiere of the China Syndrome.

This film was about a nuclear meltdown at an American power facility. During the after party the woman I was with spotted Cher sitting with songwriter Stephan Bishop. She dared me to ask Cher for a dance so I went up to her and asked. After looking me up and down Cher said yes and we hit the dance to Ami Stewarts seminal hit 'Knock on Wood'. We started doing an old sixties dance called the swim when the paparazzi clocked us, came over and started taking pictures. Cher left abruptly never to be seen again that night… but admittedly that was one dream that was perfectly fulfilled!! About a week later the Three Mile Island nuclear meltdown happened in Pennsylvania!! Talk about synchronicity!!

I worked with Ernie Glucksman and that merry bunch of show business folks for over two years. Ernie died and left a legacy of his work for me, the only stipulation was that I had to stay in LA and work with his widow and daughter. The plan was for me to do stand-up then go into film or TV. By this time I had saved enough money to go to England as Reg had invited me to come over and do some recordings with him and his brother Gus.

It was getting to that time where I really needed to decide what I wanted to do. The residue of the Los Angeles cultural wasteland intrinsically weighed upon my innate spiritual consciousness. The winds of change were inherent in every molecule of America's streets. From the renewal of incarnate gangs running the streets to the advent of nouveau designer drugs sold for pennies to unsuspecting victims of an ancient holocaust. These entities whose existence would be constantly challenged by a social order whose pungent history was rewritten to expound the glorious past of a people enslaved. A segment of society condemned to an unjust dereliction…a misnomer that slavery ended with the civil war but propagated through the justification of commercial racism. A directed mindset to humble the strongest of men destined for the annals of industrial slavery.

Chapter 5
London Calling

I took off for England in June of 1980. Reggie Isidore met me at Gatwick airport in his black Daimler. As we drove through the lush green English countryside a tear came to my eye... it was a dream come true. I stayed with Reggie and his family and sometimes with Gus and his mum. It was my first time in England but having worked with two artists from England I knew a bit about the cultural landscape of this evergreen nation.

It was a great summer of music. Gus Isidore was a bit of a child prodigy on guitar who had recorded with Marc Bolan when he was 14 years old. I had my work cut out for me... you see Gus and Reg played a hybridisation of West Indian Rhythms with a rock edge and the soul of an African drummer.

It was a challenge... so I dug deep into that place where my ancestors reside and we produced some amazing demos. Reggie said that if I decided to move to England to play with him and Gus there would probably be a management deal on offer. All this sounded good but I knew Ernie's widow was expecting me to start my career as a comedy actor. After we finished recording I left England and went back to California. After talking to my mother about the offer to do comedy as a gateway into film and TV acting my mother declared that 'I don't want anyone laughing at my son'. I decided to put acting on the back burner and move to England. I packed my things and finished the shows I had been booked to perform.

I needed to finish the demo recordings of my songs. Whilst I was working in the studio laying down backing vocals for one of my songs, the engineer announced that someone wanted to see me out the back. I stepped out of the studio and there was a long silver limousine in the alley. The tinted window came down slowly...I looked inside and it was Lee Garrat!

Lee had serendipitously heard that I was moving to England and he just wanted to covey good wishes to me and say there were no hard feelings about my band cancelling the shows we had rehearsed for. Lee knew that I wanted to do the gigs regardless of Steve and Tony who had pulled out. Lee had just scored a number one Billboard hit with Jermaine Jackson that week with 'Lets Get Serious', co-written with Stevie Wonder.

Reggie and Gus called from London to say that they had secured the management deal and I was promised a weekly wage, my own flat and a chance to record and play gigs with their new band. I was committed to this new musical constituent as my foremost disposition agreed with a need to encapsulate a fresh and creative aptitude.

My endowment from the estate of Ernest Glucksman was receded in favour of my instinctive need to placate the indigenous annals of African and West Indian rhythm. When I got to London I enjoyed the genuine Dominican hospitality of Gus Isidore and his mum, until I established residency in my own abode.

Gus's mum was awesome! She exhibited a penchant to assume a motherly disposition to each and all asunder. However she did say I had to watch out for Reggie, he had been hit in the head by a cricket ball when he was a kid and sometimes he would just do crazy things.

Gus was busy with recording sessions and gigs for various artists like *The Foundations* whilst preparing songs for our projects. I got contacted within days of arriving to do a gig with *The Marvelettes*. They were a female singing group which, boasted hits on the famed Motown label including 'Please Mister Postman' and 'Don't Mess with Bill'.

We played at the *People's Club*, which was previously called *Cue Club* a famous club in the Paddington area of west London owned by an Afro-Caribbean guy. It was an early centre of black culture in Britain. Audrienne Ferguson was the *Marvelettes'* lead singer and eventually settled in Britain.

The management company for our band was based in Southampton and headed by a chap named Mel with our tour manager Dave Poulton an ex DJ. A singer by the name of Bobby Harrison ex *Procol Harum* and *Snafu* had organised everything. We were then contracted to be his backing band. They immediately put us on a wage and I got my flat on Putney Hill in leafy southwest London. I loved this semi suburban area, it reminded me of the Wiltshire District where I had lived in Los Angeles. This place was luxurious, with a genteel environment for music practice and a great setting for furthering my own social activities.

Fumi had flown back to Japan whilst I was in LA the plan being that she would come to London once I got settled. When Fumi arrived she surprised me with my first four track portable studio! A little something she picked up in Tokyo, which was known - even then - for its cutting edge music technology. With the business sorted for management, rehearsals commenced at a farm owned by singer Micky Jupp near Chelmsford, Essex.

We stayed at a motel during the week in Brentwood a few miles from Jupp's farm and at weekends would stay in London. Management would cover everything... all we had to do was rehearse and write music.

We christened the band name as *Asia* and after several weeks of rehearsals and writing sessions it was decided we would go into a recording studio to lay down the new songs. By this time we had secured the services of an amazing synthesizer programmer named Phil

Nicolas. Jam studios was booked for the sessions. The studio was owned by *Abba* and John Etchels was the engineer. John had recorded some of *Queen's* classic albums and his recording technique for vocals was outstanding.

We enlisted the talents of Jerome Rimson in order to help produce the tracks as he had produced the *Real Things* album, which had been certified platinum. Jerome was an amazing bassist and I must say it was pretty intimidating having him in the studio.

The recording turned out great and there was talk of a deal. Then the first disaster struck. Robin Trower, Reg Isidore's old employer came to check one of our rehearsals and decided he needed Reg back to record an album with Jack Bruce from *Cream*.

Then out of the blue Gus and Bobby decided to get Jerome in to play bass and Carlton Morales to be the second guitarist. Carlton would go on to play guitar on Julian Lennon's debut album *Valotte*. Reg, Gus and I had done some gigs with Peter Green and Peter asked me to put a band together for him. Management decided to back this project as well so my salary was secure. Then everything went pear-shaped. Our management in Southampton had over stretched their funding and went bankrupt. By this time Peter Green's lawyers started to get involved and Peter told them to put us on a wage and bookkeeper Val Bain was brought in to over see the financial arrangements.

Gus did some gigs with us as did Reg and Pete Bardens from *Camel*. Reg and Pete were old mates. Pete and I ended up being good pals as well. He had remembered partying with me when I was in Eric Burdon's band as we were on the same bill for concerts on the east coast of America.

Fumi and I were starting to have problems by this time. I was under so much pressure trying to keep everything together I guess it spilled over into our relationship. There was so much politics flying about with colleagues and management…it was very strange. And as the sun would shine the next day all I wanted to do was to play music. While I was rehearsing in Southampton for a gig down there we went to a club called *Barbarellas*. I met this gorgeous English lady named Patricia who was there on a girl's night out. We fell in love… She would have a profound affect on my life. Fumi and I broke up… it was mutual. Our relationship had run its course. She dated Peter Green for a while then Fumi moved back to Tokyo to start a business and a family.

Jeff Whitaker, the percussionist in Peter Green's band decided to take over the band. We had a clash and Peter sided with Jeff for whatever reasons. I left the band… this was the beginning of 1982. When I lost my luxury flat in Putney, Pat and I had moved into a holiday flat temporarily. Then I lost my hearing due to catarrh build up in my inner ear. So I had no gig and I was deaf with a declination of no salary coming in.

Pat had gotten a job as a legal secretary, she could type ninety words a minute and encouraged to me to carry on as she could take care of us until I got better. I started to give singing lessons just to get some cash in.

I even got a job as a labourer but that only lasted a day… I wasn't into digging ditches especially in full view on the Edgeware Road in central London. I had an audition for *Climax Blues Band* but my hearing affected my playing and it was just awful I could not hear a thing. There is an old saying 'You got to go through it to get to it'.

My hearing got better as the spring of 1982 kicked in and I started doing sessions again. A Ghanaian percussionist named Lord Eric had seen me play with Peter Green and contacted me about doing a session with *Osibisa*. I turned up to the studio to see my idols *Osibisa* in the flesh; the pensive, vibey Teddy Osei, the energetic Mac Tontoh and the heartbeat of the band drummer/composer Sol Amarfio.

We recorded a version of their seminal Afro Latin hit 'Sunshine Day' and an original dance track called 'Move Your Body' complete with bass slaps and a solid bassline courtesy of me and my prototype Wal bass. I got on really well with the guys I got my double session fee and left. A couple days later I got a call from Teddy Osei asking if I would like to join the band as a European tour was starting in a couple weeks.

I took the job and Teddy put me on a small retainer although I was still doing sessions but things started to take off. My first gig with *Osibisa* was Nyon Folk Festival at which point I had never even rehearsed with the band.

I was given a tape of the songs and I had a top and tail section with Sol the drummer, which set me up quite well to handle the gigs. Sol had written some of the band most poignant songs such as 'Woyaya' and 'Welcome Home'. I did very well on that first gig holding down a solid rhythm to the mighty Osibisa rhythm section, which consisted of Daku Potato on conga, Frank Tontoh on drums along with Sol. We did a lot of TV spots & tours that year but I also managed to continue doing sessions.

I met this singer from a band called the *Members*, Nick (Nicky) Tesco. We got on real well, he liked my vibe and we started jamming with different musicians. He lived around the corner from Ladbroke Grove, which was quite bohemian in those days with lots of studios, shops, private clubs and bars. Nick put me together with *J Walter Negro;* a couple guys from NYC who had enjoyed a club hit in the UK. Walter was the rapper/graffiti artist and Leonard K Seeley was the guitarist. We would go on to record one of the first English/US rap records 'The Cost of Living' under the name of *NATO* (Negro and Tesco Organisation) and do a joint tour with the *Members*.

I'll never forget the write up for our London gig the reviewer said when we played our single the bass line just grab you by the neck and dragged you out to the dance floor. Now *that's* a write up! Nick and I would collaborate on a few projects over the years but the *NATO* project had the highest profile. We did play Womad under the band name of *BMW* (Bad Man Wagon).

This band was made up of session musicians who were from different recording acts; Claire Hirst (*Belle Stars*) was on sax, Chuck Sabo (*Shakespeare's Sister*) on drums, Nigel Bennett guitar (*The Members*), Gus Isidore (Seal) guitar, Nick and myself. This was quite an eclectic group but we only did a couple of gigs. Around this time in 1982 I met Isaac Hayes who had moved to London and as we were both from Memphis, we talked about doing a, collaboration. As I was doing projects with Nick Tesco and his management company which was ran by Ian Grant and Allan Edwards, I decided to tell them about the project with Isaac Hayes and they decided to back the recording project.

Ian and Allan were good people and were at the top of the music business. Ian handled the management and Allan did the PR. They managed *Big Country*, and *The Members* amongst others and Allan did PR for the *Rolling Stones* and David Bowie.

Isaac Hayes invited me around to his flat to discuss what track we would do I played him a couple demos of an African track and a mid tempo dark soul track. Upon on the hearing the African rhythms he said 'where is the one (the downbeat)'.

I said 'its up there (on the up beat), he loved the African rhythms but we decided to record a jazz funk track which was called 'Baby Talk'. After the meeting he made some Memphis styled fried chicken, red beans and rice topped off with some lemon meringue pie.

Isaac was a great cook and after his short stint in London he would go on to host a radio show on Kiss in New York, play Chef in South Park the animated series and star in a series of films and television programs.

When we recorded my first single 'Baby Talk' we made it a jazzy dance piece, which made British DJ Tony Blackburn's charts. But more was to come from that song 'Baby Talk a few years down the line. It was still a struggle to be a musician but things were always looking up, looking positive. I had a routine often I would get up when Pat was going to work in the Strand at the law firm. I would exercise my body… do stretches, practice reading a few charts, work on my bass technique and then work on songs. In the afternoon I would make business calls follow up calls for sessions etc.

It was the same routine I had when I was in Los Angeles however I think I was networking a lot more in London because it was all new to me. Between gigs with Osibisa and recording sessions I was kept pretty busy. In my head getting up early exercising the body, practising music reading & stamina building, having a writing session and business calls were all a part of my daily mantra.

It was a customary way of life I had been leading for years. This reinforced my spiritual being for the humility of rejection that my community of artists know only so well as this has been ingrained into the very DNA of our professional makeup for years. But repetition is good in life…. It's like playing a riff over and over you only get better at it each time.

Sometimes just putting yourself out there on the street makes things just happen. Often I would go down to Denmark Street in the West End and hang at some music shops and play on the basses. This lead to a sponsorship deal with Yamaha through the manager of one of the shops named Tony. The shop was right next to the legendary *Andy's Guitars* where many a rock star would buy or repair their guitars.

You would see Elvis Costello, Malcolm McLaren, Johnny Rotten and many of the current artists of the time. Denmark St was like the tin pan alley of London besides music stores there were also recording studios, music management offices, publishing companies and even clubs near by like the *Astoria* and the *Borderline*.

It was one of the many hubs of activity in London's music scene but albeit a major one. I kept my deal with Yamaha for at least 4 years it was mainly for music equipment and I did a few music workshops and showcases for them.

Another deal I got at the time was with Rotosound Strings I was given 60 sets of bass strings a year....well I only used maybe 10-20 sets a year the rest was profit. I learnt the power of sponsorship and how it was a viable financial stream, which sat alongside other revenue streams to be made through publishing, PRS, performing and record royalties. I learned that a musician had to be not only versatile in the types of music he played but also adapt at the business side of things if he wanted a long career. I knew the importance of publishing as an income and promotion as a vehicle to put ones music in the public domain.

The experience I was gaining in the recording studio as a songwriter and a musician led the way to me adding the role of producer to my skillset. One of the first records I produced was for the owners of Record Shack Records on Berwick Street it was for a group UK funk group based in Essex.

I tried to capture their raw funk sound but Jeff Weston and his partner wanted a club record and they got a well known DJ named Froggy to do the mix. Jeff would go on to champion Hi-energy dance music, which was supported by the pink pound.

My next production would be with *Hanoi Rocks* whom I met at a famous festival of the midnight sun near Lapland in Finland. *Osibisa* was one of the main acts but we didn't get on stage until 4am. I had a good relationship with Andy McCoy who was the leader of the band.

I produced two B-sides for their singles released on Sony Records. I even toured with them as a guest musician playing percussion and synthesizer. It was a crazy tour with support by Johnny Thunders of the *New York Dolls*. *Hanoi Rocks* would go on to have a big influence on *Guns n Roses* who in turn bought their entire catalogue. I learnt all this from their guitarist Slash, himself.

The scope of music genres I covered was quite extreme from African music, funk hip-hop, glam rock, dance and pop. Versatility was the name of the game and it was the one thing that kept me busy through the lean times.

1983 would see me touring with *Osibisa*, which culminated with a live recording and video shoot at the famous *Marquee Club* in London for their 25th anniversary. The album 'Osibisa Live at the Marquee' was released with a DVD to follow over 10 years later.

Rock and Roll and UFOs

I was quite busy in 1983 at one point I was touring with three bands *Osibisa*, *NATO* with *The Members* and Finnish singer Kojo. I spent seven weeks in Finland touring with Kojo during that summer. They got me in at the last moment as a dep.

I never had a rehearsal with the band I just listened to a tape of the album on the plane flight to Helsinki. I knew if I could sing the melodies I could play the bass to the songs. The band consisted of; Gus Isidore on guitar, Billy Carson drums, me on bass and a Latvian named Balese on piano.

When we arrived Gus and I topped and tailed the songs at the hotel. The next day we had to fly to play three festivals around Finland in one day. Even at this point in my life I had never flown to three different festivals in one day... it was full on.

Kojo was a real crazy guy who was often so drunk during our gigs that he would start abusing his fans but they loved it. I really enjoyed touring in Finland the women were quite exotic and we got some good sponsorship with companies like Levi Jeans.

I was still living with Pat in London but we came close to breaking up while I was in Finland. She came over during the last part of the tour and I had to keep a low profile... and even then I almost got into trouble when this Finnish girl who had spotted us leaving a restaurant and came running after me.

I just about got out of that one, but Pat and I decided to get married upon my return to London. However we had a great time in Helsinki it's a beautiful city. When I got back to London I was straight into tours with *Osibisa* and supporting *The Members* with Nicky Tesco and NATO. It was hectic but I loved it.

Around this time I got called to do a session with a Ghanaian singer named *Bob Pinado* he was like the James Brown of Ghana. I got to the studio & Trinidadian engineer Ben E King was producing and the rest of the band were the *Osibisa* rhythm section Kari Bannerman guitars, Emmanuel Rentzos keyboards, Daku Potato on conga. My currency as a specialist African funk bassist was definitely on the rise. We did the whole of Bob Pinado's album in six hours. My head was screwed for the next week as the concentration level to do this specific type of African music was heavy. Apparently this album did very well in Africa, although my fee was very small.

I was proud to be a part of a genre-crossed album... mixing funk and African rhythms. Now you hear Pinado's music on the *Ghana Soundz* albums, African funk from the late seventies & early eighties are in vogue amongst London's young hip set.

Between 1983-1984 I would see the releases of previous years work including: 'Osibisa Live at the Marquee', two *Hanoi Rocks* B sides, J Walter Negro & Nicky Tesco single 'Cost of Living', Leonard K. Seeley single 'Tradition' and my first solo single 'Baby Talk'. My reputation was now growing as not just a bassist, but also as a vocalist.

ABOVE: Amadou & Mariam from Mali.
BELOW: Eric Burdon on tour (me in the white hat)

A young Dominic Miller (Sting Guitarist).

ABOVE: Asia feat Gus & Reg Isidore & Bobby Harrison.
BELOW: Carlos Santana

Band with Zac Starkey, Gordon Gaynor & Chris Jagger.

The Blues Brothers

Alvin Taylor

Des'ree & Gabrielle at the Damilola Taylor Tribute

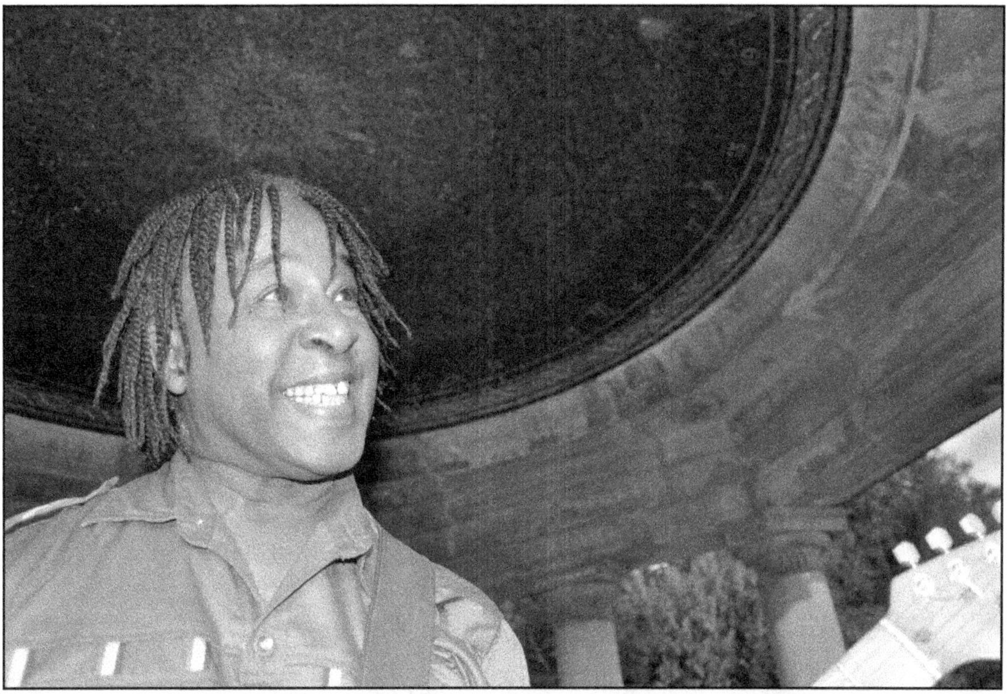

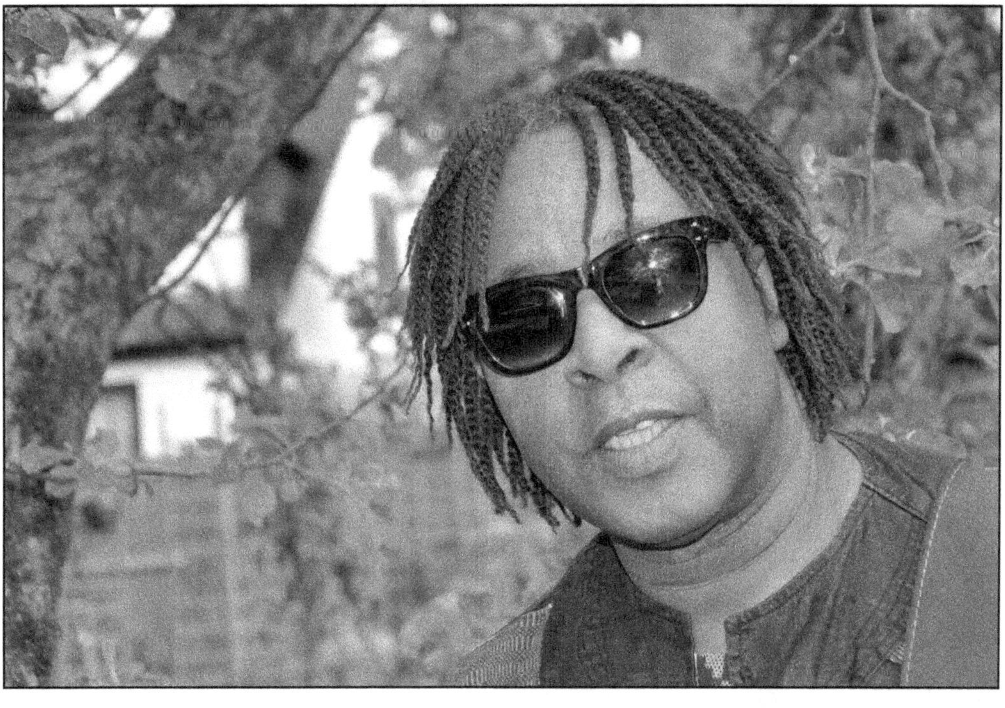

ABOVE: Finnish singer Kojo.
BELOW: The last incarnation of Osibisa

Above: In Tommy with Kim Wilde

"SIDEWALK BLUES"

"Streetcar driver" George Melly meets Greg Brown (Jelly Roll Morton) with Martin Litton and his Red Hot Peppers from *"Mr Jelly Roll - The Believe it or Not Show"* to bring Mortons' classic, Sidewalk Blues, to the streets of London.

PHOTO: PETER KEMP 071-722-6199

Isaac Hayes recording Baby Talk

Me with Baaba Maal.

ABOVE: Me, Peter Green & Gus Isidore
BELOW: Osibisa in Ghana

SPICE

BELOW: Salif Keita.

Osibisa

Playing with Red Isidore

With John 'Rabbit' Bundrick

Page 8 — SUN SOCIETY — The Senegambia Sun ♦ Monday, 7 May 1984

Senegambian Musical Festival
Lie Ngum and Highway Construction
Plus Youssou Ndure and Super Etoile

The link

AND sisterhood you might as well add, for the kinds and degree of co-operation envisaged by these two heavy brothers of Senegambian Musical entertainments are such that they call for the active involvement of all Senegambians, be they male or female, and not just as spectators — even at musical shows - but as active participants in maintaining the confederal fire burning at least in one of the most important sectors of co-operation between The Gambia and Senegal - two countries with one destiny as was so aptly symbolized at the show by the Confederal flags made out of two Gambian flags joined together at the middle by a Senegalese flag with the word "dev..." written below the star in the middle.

The Idea

The whole idea for a Senegambian Festival came about barely over a month ago when Lie Ngum, now known as Ab...

Lie Ngum or Abdel Kabir at Banjul Festival with group Highway Construction

...dium gave the necessary Confederal touch to the event.

As could be expected the show was late in starting but ...

generally, one could divide the crowd between the older men ...

crowd all got up to pay standing ovations to both Bob and Lie.

The New Lie

But before this, Lie had played his new own original songs as Abdel Kabir and all were well received by his audience. The songs were good songs in their own right and because in them Lie had achieved the difficult blend of Mbalax and funk. Lie's back up musicians did not find them difficult to execute at all. Indeed the heavy back up provided by Highway Construction and the perfect rendition of wollof songs by Lie's two chorus girls added spice to the whole thing.

The Stars Changing

Youssou Ndure also made his usual mark with The Gambian audience and even though he had performed in The Gambia only the previous week or so, he was splendidly received by the usual ladies and the rest, who could not help dancing to

The Affair (BBC)

The Affair starring Courtney Vance (lower right).

The shortlived Bad Man Wagon (BMW).

Snuffy and Ron Bushey

The Team (Warner Bros).

ABOVE: With Amanpondo at the Temple of Music in Capetown South Africa
BELOW: Yusef Latiff @ Capetown Jazz Fest.

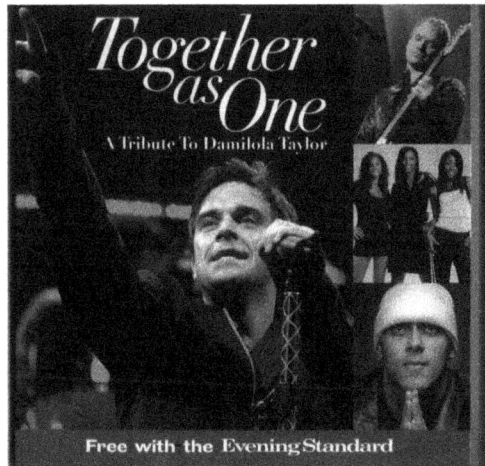
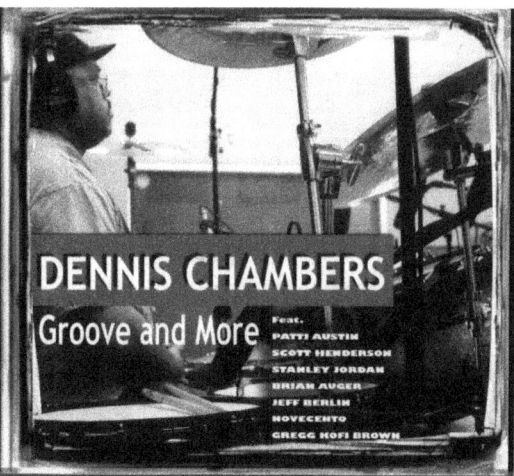

J. WALTER NEGRO
NICKY TESCO

CO$T OF £IVING

MARTA ULAETO
FRICA RISE

The Love Songs — Peter Hammill

LEGENDS OF ROCK

Osibisa LIVE

INCLUDES FREE CD

DVD [plus] **COLLECTORS EDITION** DVD VIDEO

Chapter 6
African Vibes

1984 was again a landmark year I hadn't struck gold yet but it wasn't for the lack of trying. I fell out with my heroes *Osibisa* or they fell out with me but my wife Pat was pregnant and I was not going to sit around feeling sorry for myself I had to make some money quick. Kari Bannerman called me about a gig in Bristol he had recommended me for. It was for an Pan African Caribbean dance group called *Ekome* - their drummers had appeared on the Peter Gabriel 4 'Security' album.

I met the director of *Ekome Arts* Barry Anderson who was a very astute Jamaican businessman, dancer, percussionist and producer. We got on very well so he hired me as a bassist for *Ekome*. This job would involve playing live gigs but more importantly we would be recording an album of African music with Ghanaian master drummer and composer Nii Ashitey as a guest artist. Nii Ashitey was leader of the legendary Ghana band *Wulomei*. Barry Anderson put me on a weekly retainer although I only needed to be up in Bristol where they were based for maybe two weeks out of a month.

Having me on a retainer really meant I was on call for whenever *Ekome* needed me. They were a great bunch of people and I got to discover the Bristol social scene. This scene would produce artists like *Massive Attack, Portishead*, Tricky and a street artist named Banksy.

The *Ekome* band included the legendary horn section that featured on many *Aswad* albums this was: Vin Gordon, Michael Bamy Rose and Eddie 'Tan Tan' Thornton. These guys had been around a long time, and helped to develop bluebeat music which was a precursor to Ska and reggae.

I was very lucky to be working with Vin, Mike and Tan Tan. They taught me bass lines from the old Ska and reggae songs and this grounded me for work I would do in the future. This horn section, were as tight as the Phoenix Horns (*Earth Wind & Fire*, Phil Collins). Mike had also played in one of my favourite bands from the seventies called *Cymande* - they were like a Caribbean *Mandrill*.

Rock and Roll and UFOs

The *Ekome* album was recorded at Crescent Recording Studios in Bath. Barry Anderson made me line manager of the project. As this was an album of songs and rhythms from Ghana I needed to find a keyboard player who understood the nuances of the genre.

That meant sacking the keyboard player in the band because all he could seem to play was reggae. I called my old friend Delipes who had played and recorded with lots of highlife and Afro-beat bands. This personnel change made production run smoother and more efficient as the sessions ran over a course of 3 days.

The studio was, owned by David Lord, who had produced Peter Gabriel. He looked in on us a couple times as he was intrigued by the music. David asked me one day if I knew Mark King as he wanted a slap bassist and after hearing me play thought I might know him. My reply was 'Why would you want Mark King when you got me right here?' Well he agreed, and hired me to come back the following week to play on a track by Pete Hammill from *Van der Graaf Generator*. Now as far as progressive rock goes he was a big influence on *Genesis* and Peter Gabriel.

Mr Hammill was a complete English gentleman… from the old school, and the session went very well… as a matter of fact the engineer bought the fretless Yamaha bass I was using on the *Ekome* session. Yamaha sent me up a bunch of music gear from their factory in Bletchley near Milton Keynes. So besides the bass they sent a DX7 digital synth, a digital delay unit, a bass amplifier and another fretless bass. Like I said sponsorship is as important to musicians as it is to athletes. It was an honour to guest on Pete Hammill's album alongside Brian Eno and Robert Fripp. I told Pete how much I liked Bath even though I had been stopped by the Old Bill (the police) a week earlier, when I was recording with *Ekome*.

I guess the cops weren't used to seeing so many people of colour. It seems they were looking for a black man who had robbed a shop and he was wearing blue boots and I just happen to be wearing blue boots at the time. I actually got the boots from a sponsorship deal when I was in Finland. Anyway the cops followed me into Crescent Studios where Barry and David explained that I was producing a record at the time of the crime. We had a laugh about it…I mean what are the odds of two random black geezers both wearing blue boots in Bath.

I still think it was a setup. It happened to me once before… I was accused by the Wimbledon Police Department of trying to hit someone with my car. They had my license number and everything but I showed them my passport because on the alleged date of the crime I was in Germany on tour.

Another project around this time that was to have an amazing affect on me was a tour to Gambia and Senegal playing with Gambian singer Abdul Khabir with co-support from a singer named Youssou N'Dour.

It was called the 'Highway Reconstruction Tour' and it was my first time in Africa. The rhythm section was made up of; Billy Carson on drums, Gus Isidore on guitar, a Finnish keyboard player and me on bass. We had a horn section, which included Anita Carmichael and two backing singers. This was my first time in Africa so I arranged for half my fees to be paid in advance as I had a pregnant wife. We co-headlined the gigs with Youssou N'Dour who had a cracking band with Jimmy M'Baye on guitar, Boubucar on percussion, Habib Faye on bass. Habib was about nineteen at the time but he would go on to produce Youssou N'Dour

Indeed, as I was to learn twenty-two years later when I was studying for my Masters degree in Media and Cultural studies, the governments of Senegal and France were investing money and resources into artists and producers like Youssou N'Dour to help development and maintain the indigenous music of Senegal such as Mbalax.

The main influence on Senegalese music previously was Afro Latin music and rhythm and blues. This can heard listening to bands like *Orchestra Bao*bab…it's a perfect example as you hear the Cuban rhythms play against the melody sung in Wolof. They have a distinct sound as distinct as the music of *Super Etoile de Dakar*, which is the band Youssou made his name with as a young griot.

I mean I had never heard of Youssou N'Dour before the tour and he practically owned a whole city block in Dakar. He was a big star in Senegal and Gambia but he had a bit of success in France as well. He even bought the PA system, which was shipped over from Finland for the tour. But France and Senegal wanted to stave off western influence on Senegalese music culture and create their own stars.

When I got back to London I met Peter Gabriel at the Nelson Mandela Birthday tribute at Wembley Stadium and I gave him a video of Youssou N'Dour and the Dance Troupe of Senegal. Then musical history was made. Peter Gabriel went to Senegal, to met Youssou N'Dour. Youssou and members of his band were then invited to record and tour with Peter Gabriel.

Afterwards Youssou N'Dour recorded 'Seven Seconds' with Neneh Cherry. It was fitting that his first global hit would be about a child being born as the child mortality rate in that part of the world is extremely high. Those guys give thanks to the creator everyday just for being born in this world.

The first time I heard Youssou's backing band *Super Etoile de Dakar* I was blown away. We were playing mostly footballs stadiums built by the Chinese filled to capacity with the Wolof people from Senegal and Gambia. They were one people one tribe separated by borders put up by Europeans. Senegal was a French colony and Gambia was an English colony. All in all it was a unique experience even though we only got half the money promised on the tour. Upon my arrival in London I had to get my hustle back on…my wife was about to give birth to my first child. And on September 12 six days after my mum's birthday my son Aaron was born.

I helped with the delivery however the doctor accidentally sowed the placenta back into the womb and Pat had to be rushed back into hospital! She came back after a few days but it was a close call believe me. We were amazed at the beauty of this little mixed race baby who was born into a world full of hope for the future.

Rock and Roll and UFOs

I finished up the year on tour with African jazz saxophonist George Lee who played in Johnny Nash's band 'Sons of the Jungle'. George had played in the band with Bob Marley and John 'Rabbit' Bundrick. He was a consummate jazz musician who could play anything.

If you listen to 'Natty Dread' by Bob Marley you can hear George's soloing skills. I learnt so much from George... although he could look intimidating I would always challenge him...to say I was a legend in my mind would be an under statement. Music interaction is all about inspiring your fellow musicians on to greater heights through mesmerising telepathic communication, which creates the magic!

George's album was called 'Anancy' which meant spider in Ghana. The band was made up of a drummer, two percussionists Baba Adesose Wallace and Mamadi, a guitarist, George on sax and me on bass. We did a winter tour in Scotland it was cold! But the music was hot!

By 1985 things were a bit tough. I got a few sessions, continued doing shows with *Osibisa* and local gigs with Dominic Miller. Everyone was saying don't worry, it will happen, baby's bring you luck and boy did I need luck. However I did have records coming out on major labels so I decided that I needed a publishing deal. First I had to do some solo gigs in Holland set up by a guy who apparently drank up my wages before I could get to Holland. Once I got there I had to renegotiate my fees. It was cool and around this time I met a promoter named Rob Dingshof. I played clubs near The Hague and Rotterdam.

The highlight was playing a festival supporting a girl band called *Centrefold*. They were all models that posed nude in gentlemen's magazines. And I had to share a trailer with them! Don't worry - when they got changed I picked up a magazine and keep my eyes on the pages LOL.

The next step in London was to secure publishing, meanwhile there was a management deal on the table and an album to do in October. Chappell Music publishing had expressed strong interest in the releases I had coming out. I ran into Jeff Chegwin who was A&R for Chappell. He was excited about me working with *Hanoi Rocks*.

Jeff was cool and had great energy his brother was British TV present Keith Chegwin and their sister Janice Long was a famous BBC Radio DJ. So I got the contract from the legal department at Chappell and dropped it by my solicitor to have a look. George Lee was producing an album for Nigeria Independence funded by the Nigerian Oil Company. He wanted me on board as bassist and Nigerian percussionist Remi Kabaka would play drums. It was an intense session George even had a South African bassist waiting in the wings on the first day.

It was great playing with Remi Kabaka, I knew him from LA, and had never played with him but we really locked in the studio. So the other bassist had to go home and the artist Marthe Ulato hired me to contract the backing singers for the session.

This was one of the best paid sessions ever for me anyway, and to be recording at Abbey Road Studios was an absolute thrill! Martha and George were very happy with my bass and backing vocal work but to receive £1500 for the weeks session work was for me incredible. The next day after the session I went to Chappell and struck a development publishing for £5,000. So that week I clocked up £6500… not bad for a weeks work in 1985. All the networking and discipline imprinted into my daily mode of existence was starting to pay off.

Within weeks I started getting calls from Lenny in New York saying that he's been hearing my song on the radio. Suddenly I started getting calls from the same publishing companies who had turned down my song 'Baby Talk' three years previously.

Chapter 7
Number 1 in America!

The word was out that an unknown Italian singer named Alisha had covered my song and it was getting massive airplay in the US. The producer was Mark Berry and the remix was by Shep Petibone, known for his work with Madonna. I had licensed the song to Ram Records who had released my version and there were rumours that Rob from Ram Records tried to do an illegal deal with my copyright of the song. However I knew my rights to the song were safe. So I decided to take my wife Pat and baby Aaron to America…to California to meet my Mum and my siblings.

While we were in the US I popped over to New York to meet my manager Mike who had setup a meet with the record's producer and the artist Alisha. I can't remember what producer Mark Berry was like but he must have been lucky! Alisha and her mum met Mike and I at a restaurant in the Village.

She was so excited to see me and to thank me. Then Alisha came over and whispered to me 'It's gonna be number one in two weeks time.' Well…this would definitely start the New Year off with a bang! And it came to pass that everything I had worked for… had come into fruition. 'Baby Talk' was officially number one in the US Billboard Dance charts.

After learning the original publisher at Ram Records was less than kosher, (and this was from several sources including Universal Music) I knew I needed a fresh publishing deal for 'Baby Talk' so I turned to Universal. The deal was fifty percent at source, which meant that no matter what territory the royalties came from I would get my fifty percent publishing royalty. I did the original deal for twenty five percent and realised Universal would have to buy out Ram Records so I offered Universal the extra twenty five percent for publishing.

It seems like I was just giving away publishing royalties however I realised that the more they owned publishing wise the more they would work the title. Which they did! That song was in the *Billboard* charts for three years. It had been covered by a Japanese artist and featured in the Bruce Willis detective series *Moonlighting*.

I got a very large advance for my publishing deal with Universal. Then Dominic Miller came

Rock and Roll and UFOs

to me with a gig offer in Bergen, Norway for a month so I took it. It would be a great opportunity for Dominic and I to get real tight as a unit. And tight we got.

We had spent a few years playing wine bars mainly places in and around Chelsea. But we had fun and it kept our chops up. I was busy doing my record business thing, which was starting to happen and I would do any tours that would come up. The Bergen trip was a chance to get away and play music, and there were, some good things on the horizon. So Dominic Miller, a drum machine and I started our residency gig at a smoky pub on Bergen's waterfront.

After a few days of playing we were actually starting to get noticed by the local music community. We got approached by a drummer and keyboard player who said they could organise a concert at a local venue that would pay 20 times what we were making at the pub gig we were doing. So we said yes please and started rehearsals. We were joined by, an amazing Yugoslav sax player. It looked like it was going to be a great gig. Unfortunately the manager the of the pub saw the advertising for the gig we were doing.

He called a meeting with Dominic and myself and basically said if we went ahead with the gig that we would be fired from the pub gig. I told the manager I thought we were in Norway not Russia. He went on the defence saying Norway is not like Russia. I told him we were definitely doing the gig as I had already lost my voice once during our tenure in their smoky pub.

He compromised with us... so we stopped playing the pub but we were allowed to stay at the company flat until our flight home the day after the gig. Later that night Dominic got a strange call from his wife asking if we were alright as a radioactive cloud was passing over Bergen coming from an explosion in a nuclear reactor in a place called Chernobyl in Russia! It is fair to say we were definitely intact and went on to play an amazing gig with these local musicians. The event was documented by great reviews in the Bergen press. As a matter of fact several venues clubbed together to get Dominic Miller and myself back to play Bergen during the Eurovision Song Contest, which, was being held in that city. The venues went all out to promote Dominic and I playing during the Melody Grand Pre, the daily advertisement in the press featured my picture everyday

We played at three different venues... the band was so tight many of the Eurovision folk came down for the funk. Thank god for the mindset of our international community of musicians. When ever a hot new musical talent comes to town the word usually goes out amongst local musicians first, spreading like wildfire.

Musicians are very supportive of each other in terms of buying music and going to gigs. Everything was going brilliantly... however I did have to visit the Bergen General Hospital again and this time not for losing my voice in a smoky pub. I had befriended one gorgeous lady whose boyfriend was a black belt and worked on the oil platforms. In a typical non-jealous Nordic frame of mind, the guy insisted that I let his girlfriend look after me while he was away working on an oil platform in the North Sea. Who was I to say no... it would have been an insult. So I humbly obliged.

As she was leaving my hotel room one night, I escorted her down to the lobby in my bathrobe. The hotel desk clerk made a comment to her in Norwegian. Now I don't speak the language… but I know an insult when I hear one.

I told him not talk to her and he started being aggressive to me… then he pushed me. I grabbed an adding machine and hit him in the side with it. He came around the desk and tried to tackle me. I hit my ribs and was winded. Then I panicked. I didn't want to get my ass kicked way over in Bergen Norway. I shifted gears and put my elbow to the side of his head, he was tall but he dropped and I kicked him in his ass!

When the police came I was in a daze. I looked around… we had completely destroyed the lobby of the hotel. My lady friend told the police what had happened with the desk clerk. The police asked me if I wanted to go to jail or go to bed. I opted for bed but I couldn't get out of bed the next day as I had sustained a broken rib during the battle.

As a footnote I might add that when the poor receptionist who happened to be an ex-paratrooper got out of hospital there were numerous musicians and fans who vowed to have a word with him including my lady friend's boyfriend…the black-belt. Ouch! My reputation for being a hothead precedes me. I don't believe in violence, I believe in defence and the passion in my being is just extremely strong. I can be a tad over-emotional.

Dominic Miller and I were song-writing partners. When I eventually signed up with Chappell Music as my publishers I would get Dominic in to record demos of our tunes. He would often come to me with these amazing pieces of music that I was suppose to write words to. I would ask Dom to teach me the song or run the chords by me. I would then take over half the chords out to match my melody and hook lines. Everyone says Dominic did his apprenticeship with me and I say maybe as far as the music business and writing songs… but he was already a serious musician when we first met.

As a founding member of UK funk band *Level 42* Dominic Miller was well versed in the funk, could read and play classical and Latin music. It was his versatility that I thought was useful as song-writing partner. The fact that Dominic has gone on to write and record hits for Sting makes me feel exonerated in my choices of whom I have worked with. I got Dominic signed to his first major publishing deal, when I signed with Universal. That was me being loyal… not just looking after myself.

I met *Simple Minds* drummer Mel Gaynor through a mutual friend named Mackey who had recorded with the *Thompson Twins*. Although Mel and I were destined to record together eventually we initially just hung out together.

We generally went to a place off Southampton Row in London called *Brown's* where you would bump into the likes of George Michael or David Bowie on the dance floor. Another place we went to was called the *Limelight* where I remember meeting record label impresario Seymour Stein, actor Dolph Lundgren and members of *U2* with assorted celebrities and hangers on.

I went to *Music Me*ss in Frankfurt with Mel where we had a bit of a blow as he liked my bass playing. Legendary drummer Billy Cobham was there, I had only recently met him in New York. Mel introduced us and Billy asked me 'Weren't we suppose to work together?'

Actually I had told Mel I turned down a chance to produce Billy when 'Baby Talk' was a hit. I couldn't see myself telling my hero what to play. Mel was impressed anyway and asked me to accompany him on bass at a drumming concert he was doing in Edinburgh, Scotland!

It was amazing to play with Mel Gaynor he is such a powerhouse on the kit and we were playing *Mahavishnu Orchestra*, Billy Cobham and Herbie Hancock. However Mel was such a cheeky bugger. He would catch your eye while you were playing then really start grooving… once he has you in the pocket he would turn the beat around. So what was the downbeat suddenly became the upbeat. Mel got me once but never again; for the rest of the gig I just concentrated on my grooves.

I really enjoyed the fruits of my hit record during this time. Pat could be a full time mum Aaron was growing into an adorable good-natured boy. I was still doing sessions and getting the odd cover. One team I worked with was twins *Molly and Polly* with Andy Longhurst as engineer producer. Molly and Polly became really good friends and were based in Ladbroke Grove where we would visit during the carnival season.

My next project was to be in Holland working with a singer named Glenda Peters she was from Surinam but grew up in the Netherlands. My friend Rob Dingsoff whom I had met on my previous outing there as a solo artist did the deal for me. Glenda had won a singing contest on Dutch TV talent contest called *Sound Mix Show* hosted by Henny Huisman, he was a household name and Glenda became a sensation over night.

Her style was very much in the vein of Randy Crawford. I spent two or three weeks working with her, the record company hired me a cottage at a classy holiday resort. I got two ladies to come and keep me company one from Norway and the other a Swiss girl who lived in New York. My energy level was high and my soul had a vacuum that needed to be filled. I needed to subdue any negative vibes in my creative space and mind before it could reach critical mass. I needed people I could trust in my inner circle and I needed an entourage for show but mainly to keep people at bay. This was show business baby!

We were invited to a host of media parties in Holland. On one occasion my girls and I along with my sponsors set off for Hilversum, which was a media centre for the whole of the Netherlands. I was taken on the set of the *Henny Huisman's Sound Mix Show* where I got to meet the man himself. The show was produced by Dutch media giants Endemol of *Big Brother* fame.

This media centre was like combining the BBC with ITV or NBC with ABC… it was huge! The press was on hand interviewing me as producer of Glenda Peters' new single. Then, the rumours started about me by an independent Dutch label owner. Despite my being accompanied by two women wherever I went. This guy was quoted in the press saying that I was gay. It was a hilarious story and made for good copy.

Rob Dingsoff and fellow Dutch businessman Daniel Lyondijk invited me to make a trip to New York and LA in order to introduce them to contacts for bringing acts to Holland. New York was great for the hang but my real strong contacts were in LA. Upon arrival to Los Angeles I introduced them to Norm Winter who I had known since I promoted the Elton John gig as he had been the PR guy.

Now Norm worked for Michael Jackson as his PR guru. Norm was a nice guy and struck a partnership with my Dutch contacts Rob and Daniel. Daniel Lyondijk would be my long-term friend, colleague and advisor, until his death in January 2011.

Meanwhile music technology was surging ahead... when I produced Glenda Peters I brought my own sequencer in the form of the Yamaha CX5 music computer and the RX11 drum machine. But samplers were now being used in ways people never dreamed and digital recording was just around the corner. Unfortunately for me I had made a detour to Norway to see one of my girls when I went to Holland and my wife Pat found the flight ticket and her woman's instinct took over...I didn't have a chance.

We decided to separate the next year in 1988 but in the mean time I would see out the end of 1987 by touring in Australia, Sri Lanka and Thailand. I made sure Pat had loads of cash from my publishing company when I hit the road. Around this time I had just signed a record deal with Magnet Records to front a band called *The Team*. This was a studio band that had been fronted by *Light of the World* and *Incognito* founder member Paul 'Tubbs' Williams. Gee Bello who had taken over the helm for 'Light of the World', apparently had the rights to *The Team* brand as well.

It was a fun project and Mel Gaynor played drums on the sessions. I played a bit of bass, sang lead vocals and played some guitar. We recorded The JB's classic 'Breaking Bread' and two original titles. Because it was with friends I didn't handle the business as tight as I normally would have. As a matter of fact the deal cost me £500. It's the first time I ever paid to sign a record contract.

Gordon Gaynor, Mel's brother was brought in to play guitars and Jimmy for percussion and vocals. I heard Gee had taken the advance for studio costs. I wasn't happy about what happened and by the time the record came out I had gotten Jimmy on the *Osibisa* tour and we were on the road. Australia was amazing... the gigs were great and the ladies were very receptive. It was my first trip and I was in full party mode. I met up with Bowie guitarist Carlos Alomar when I was invited to see David Bowie's 'Glass Spider Tour'.

Carlos and I hit the bars after the gig and started drinking Raging Bulls. This drink was named after Stephanie LaMotta daughter of boxer Jake Lamotta from the film 'Raging Bull'. Stephanie and Julian Lennon used to date and it was during their time together that this drink was created.

I forgot what was in the Raging Bull but the bartender would set it on fire and you had to blow it out and drink it in one gulp. Anyway after about four of these drinks I passed out. When I came to I was in bed in my hotel room but…I had company and she was about four times my size. Carlos had set me up!!

To make matters worse the band, were all waiting for me, as we had to fly off to do some gigs near Melbourne. Anyway I asked the young lady to leave first but everyone clocked that she had left my room. I denied anything happened and our percussionist Potatoe asked me if I had her telephone number.

He liked his women big! Australia was an awesome place! We played places like Port Macaury, Cuff's Harber, Twin Towns (Surfers Paradise), Melbourne (Swagman's) and Sydney. We flew over the Great Barrier Reef, communed with nature in this geographical paradise, and sought out redemption through coitus with the many goddesses that inhabited this fair land. It was basically a tour of RSL clubs, which were for retired servicemen clubs but open to the public.

Aside from the exotic ladies one of my fondest memories was after a particular exciting gig in Twin Towns, Surfers Paradise. A shy little Aborigine man and his family came up to me after seeing the response *Osibisa*, an African band, got from the Anglo Australians. In no uncertain terms he told me he really enjoyed the gig and… I made him proud to be black. Considering you could kill an Aborigine legally if he stepped on your property as recently as the 1950s, this meant a lot to me and reminded me why I was in this business in the first place; to make a difference and further impact the social consciousness of my audience, was always my dream and focus.

When I recount the narrative that drove my career it won't be the superfluous successes encumbered by ones account balance or ones little black book. My memories will be stilled on the affect my music had on people; the epiphany of an Aborigine who discovered pride in the tone of his skin. The skinhead who jettisons years of racist venom after hearing the conscious lyrics of an African band.

Our next stop would be Sri Lanka but we made a detour to Thailand. We had time to kill and what better place to do it in? I'm not even going say what happened during the six days of our rest and recuperation time in Bangkok, however precise it to say I enjoyed it thoroughly. Sri Lanka was another story… we went there for twelve days to raise awareness and money for the orphans of a very long war. I forged a relationship immediately with the singer who worked in the lounge of the Ramada hotel where we were staying in Colombo, Sri Lanka. Her name was Ramona and she was a very beautiful Sri Lankan lady who also lived in Los Angeles. She kept me fully occupied and acquainted me with the local cuisine which was very spicy curry based food.

Meanwhile Jimmy had forged a partnership with a gang of jewellers. They took him out to the jungle to go through a ritual, which apparently included jumping off a waterfall, picking the hair out an elephant's ass and digging up as many sapphires as you can carry.

Jimmy came back with loads of rubies, sapphires and semi-precious and precious stones. It was like he hit the jackpot I don't know how he did it. He had just done a stretch in prison when I met him, but he definitely knew something I didn't know. However Jimmy was generous and shared out the stones amongst all the band members.

Jimmy started showing an interest in Ramona so I just stepped back and started a relationship with the assistant tour manager named Libby - she was sweet, safe and British. It's so easy to get caught up in jealous scenarios when touring on the road with a band but its all an illusion. It's all a temporary façade not to be taken at face value because the face is not real! When the dream ends and the cloud clears you can find yourself in a very dark place if your premonitions are not heeded.

All in all we did some good works in Sri Lanka, we played two big concerts with an audience of at least ten thousand people each time. Visiting the ghettos of Sri Lanka was heart rendering however we played for the president and did some smaller gigs for the Lion's Club, the charity we were working with.

The mass consciousness was raised along with a whole lot of money. My stance, whilst being entertained by the upper classes in Colombo Sri Lanka, was that 'I was there on behalf of the poor and destitute. Those were the people I would make time for.'

Chapter 8
Life Changes

Back in London I had purchased a new flat and kitted it out with a demo studio. I was ready for my new life as a single man. You know if you are used to having people in your life it can be a difficult change if you suddenly find yourself living alone. Its like you have to get to know yourself all over again. It can be a difficult transition especially if you are far away from your family.

I stayed focused for the most part but I did some things I shouldn't' have done. Hung around some people I shouldn't have but all in all the opportunities just kept coming. I got a distribution deal for a house record I had recorded and first indications from DJ reports were very positive. I hadn't had a solo project released in seven years I was well pleased. It was a good time.

I spent the next year finding myself. Pat had moved back to Southampton and we had arranged that I would see Aaron on Sundays if I was in town. In the mean time I started an affair with this crazy Anglo South African girl named Paula.

Osibisa called me for a European Tour so I decided to do some merchandising with *Osibisa* tee shirts. I had one thousand shirts printed up and took Paula along to handle the sales. I got sponsorship with Casio for guitars and keyboards and a deal with Premiere drums for the tour.

We must have travelled over twenty thousand miles through Europe during the summer of 1989. The mini van was uncomfortable but the hotels were great and the gigs were amazing! It was the last time we were to play in a divided Germany as the walls came down after our tour that year.

Having a girlfriend on tour was a blessing and a curse but it was, all good, in the end. I will say that at the end of the tour there was a deficit and most of the musicians did not get their full money. I got all my money because I had the merchandise and the sponsorship so I knew what was happening with the finances and the promoters.

I had elevated myself beyond just being a musician…I was also part of the music business. I knew how it worked since I booked Elton John all those years ago. I knew I wanted a change from the music business; it wasn't nice to see people getting ripped off... even if I got paid. But things were going to change, there was something waiting for me just around the corner.

Earlier that year I did a TV commercial for Panasonic TV, it was a vocal session with my old mate Bobby Tench (who had sang on two Jeff Beck albums), Lance Ellington and myself. I hit some pretty high falsetto parts during the recording and got called back to do some additional dialogue for the commercial. This job had led me to join Equity, the actors union.

A writer approached Bobby Tench about doing a play about Jellyroll Morton however he turned it down. Then Bobby said I would be perfect for the job. The writer got in touch with me. I did a reading and got the part to play Jellyroll Morton. I had trained to do musical comedy theatre before I left LA so this was a kind of fate... it was meant to happen.

I studied for two months learning my lines working with a director and starting rehearsals. I was lucky to be looking after my solicitor's farm near Ipswich in Suffolk at the time. It was a great environment for studying a play. I recorded a cassette tape of me reading the dialogue and would listen to it constantly even in my sleep.

My debut was at the Bude Jazz Festival on the beautiful north Cornwall coast. I would be performing at a venue in the hotel where I would be staying. I had to do 2 two hour shows back to back... my first acting job in England. I had learnt seventy-five pages of dialogue, the guy interviewing me as Jellyroll only had to recite his dialogue from the book.

There was a tricky moment during one scene where I had to play a bit of piano whilst engaging in a witty repartee... After the two shows all my nerves went to my legs and I couldn't walk. Lucky for me Paula was there to help...all in all I did well and earned a lot of loyal fans. Looks like my wish for a change came just in time. The opportunity presented itself, I answered the call and was ready for action. Only through sheer discipline was I able to pool my latent knowledge together and focus the skills I had to manifest for an audience. I got an acting agent and had only one more music project to do before embarking on my new career.

I met a nice kid at the airport on my return from a holiday. His name was Tim Simenon... as a DJ/producer he had produced a hit with Nenah Cherry called 'Buffalo Stance'. Tim's moniker was 'Bomb the Bass' and he invited me to his studio for a writing session.

It was a very laid back, no pressure type of session with the odd spliff being passed about. I played bass, guitar and did the backing vocals with Noel McCalla on lead vocals and Tim doing the beats and samples. We normally did three days in a week in the studio.

The other days Tim was working with his then girlfriend Kat, the dancer from Prince's band. Tim also had projects ongoing with the members of *Tackhead*: Doug Wimbush, Skip McDonald and Adrian Sherwood. They were the Sugar Hill Label rhythm section in New York back in the day. Doug, Skip and Adrian had played on a lot of hit records.

Things were going good Rhythm King Records loved the work I was doing with Tim and they were talking to me about a five album record deal. In the studio next door S Express were recording... Mark and Sonique had heard me playing and wanted me for their band. I turned down their offer, as I wanted to finish my work with Tim and sort out a record deal for myself. Having recently received a particularly large royalty check from the Performing Rights Society I mentioned this to Tim but he had never heard of PRS. I was stunned...I told him that performing rights royalties were a big part of a songwriter's revenue stream and it's a guaranteed pension.

I obviously unknowingly stepped on some toes...I didn't know the ins and outs of Tim's business dealings but something was not right. It could have been an oversight, I remember when I played with Pete Green his lawyers found over a quarter million dollars of unpaid royalties from PRS and that was just from 'Black Magic Woman' alone! However something was amiss! Suddenly I started getting the cold shoulder from the record company Rhythm King. Then I stopped getting calls from Tim. I didn't have time to worry about this as I had a private audition that my acting agents had set me up with.

David Leland who had written *Personal Services* starring Julie Walters and directed *The Big Man* which starred Liam Neeson was to direct a stage version of *The Blues Brothers*. It was not an adaptation of the film but more of a British imagining of the film. I remembered the film... Wayne Anthony who sang with my band had a bit part in the gospel section with James Brown and Rev James Cleveland's choir.

For my audition I decided to do a James Brown dance routine whilst singing 'Midnight Hour'. I did my side shuffles and glides and I sang, I was having fun... the audition didn't matter. I ended my routine with a splits I got a good reaction from the audition team but it was David Leland's daughters who were blown away by my performance. And I got the gig! The first day of rehearsals was more of a workshop with improvisation and some tried and tested dialogue by Con O'Neal who played Jake and Warwick Evans who played Elwood. I was cast as a Bluette along with Kwame Kwei–Armah (formerly known as Ian Roberts) and Liza Spenz. So with a small cast of five and the band onstage I knew this was going to be a very busy show for the performers.

The rehearsals went very smoothly... the band knew their stuff. Tony McCormick the bandleader had played a version of the show with Con and Warwick at a pub in Brighton and the *Hampstead Theatre* in London. We all contributed, bits and pieces to the show. To tighten up the rough edges they got in Carol Todd for the choreography. I added a Bobby McFerrin style vocal bass line to accompany Kwame's amazing rendition of 'Under the Boardwalk', which went down well and they made my James Brown audition piece part of the show.

The previews went down a storm. In the beginning only Kwame and I received rave reviews in the press but as the news went around all the reviews came in and the critics seemed to love it. I remember one preview in particular a benefit for 'The Friends of John McCarthy' who was being held hostage in the Lebanon. Well, as providence would have it, John McCarthy was freed on the day of the show so the evening turned into an amazing celebration in honour

Rock and Roll and UFOs

of his release. It was as if all the stars had aligned at the right time to bestow a blessing on this production.

From then on everyone wanted a piece of *A Tribute to the Blues Brothers* and so many people and celebrities would show up backstage or at the stage door wanting to meet the actors. It was an incredible feeling. Unfortunately for us the theatre was at the back of number 10 Downing Street, home of the Prime Minister. One Saturday during the end of a matinée show we had a bomb scare. The IRA apparently attempted to bomb Downing Street. We got the all clear to go back to the theatre for the evening show. Singing 'Two Little Boys', a wartime song from the First World War took on a poignant meaning that night, as we sang defiantly to the military beat.

Performing eight shows a week… day in and day out… can take its toll so I set up a little gym in one of the unused dressing rooms complete with exercise bike, re bounder and exercise mat. I would get to the theatre early and do 45min to an hour workout everyday then take some rescue remedy to keep my energy up for the show. This was my first long term run in a theatre so the lifestyle and social scene was new to me. Kwame Kwei-Armah would have his head deep into writing plays or marketing and selling merchandise for Spike Lee. He grew up in Southall and at that time when it was very hard for black people in Britain.

His parents put him through private theatre school, so although Kwame could talk the West Indian patois he was very adapt with the Queens English as well. I knew he was sharp and would be a force to be reckoned with in the future. He was very helpful to me as a dressing roommate and would give me tips on improving my stage performance. Kwame would go on to star on Brit TV hit *Casualty*, and become part of Britain's black intelligentsia as a panellist on UK TV arts programmes. He is only the second black playwright in UK history to have a production in London's West End. Kwame is now artistic director at Baltimore's Centre Stage Theatre in the USA.

Con O'Neal and Warwick Evans had both starred in another hit play called *Blood Brothers* so we became quite close to some of the actors from that show. Michael Ball, Pauline Quirke, Prince and Princess Michael of Kent were just some of the celebrities that came to pay homage to the show. My best moment came when Sean Connery showed up with his family and demanded to meet me, Liza and Kwame. I was so thrilled to meet my hero James Bond and I gave him a big hug. Well it turned out that he was our executive producer… as it was his money that went into the show's production.

Being used to routines and discipline I was able to make the transition from music to theatre actor, which very few musicians had been able to do up to that point. Everything was going perfectly at this time it seems I had the world in the palm of my hands. But you know sometimes when you are on top, things can happen to bring you right back to reality.

Even with my busy schedule I still made time to see my son Aaron every Sunday. Pat and I had a great laugh when she told me that she had seen me on TV, performing a song from the

Rock and Roll and UFOs

Blues Brothers on Terry Wogan's BBC show. I think Pat was proud of me... even though we were separated we were still fond of each other. Pat was always supportive no matter what I did. I remember when she brought my son Aaron to see me play Jellyroll at the Royal Court Theatre in London.

She was amazed to see me perform in this legendary theatre using skills that were foreign to her. Up to that point I had just been a musician to her. One day I went down to Southampton to pickup my son and I noticed Pat was wearing a wig. I asked what was happening and she said she had cancer...I almost fell over and had to steady myself. Even though we were separated I still loved her and she was the mother of my son. She said she was receiving treatment, I told her I needed to know the truth. I asked how much time she had left, she said six months to a year. But unfortunately she died two weeks later.

I was devastated, her sister, had instigated a divorce, which came to me on the day Pat died. My poor son Aaron had witnessed his mum's quick demise and her sister Pam was given custody of my son. This arrangement kind of suited me as I buried myself into work forgoing the grieving process. Then the South African girl I was dating left me for another guy and it just seemed no matter how hard I tried to lift myself up something was waiting to knock me back down.

But I grew up in racist America in the fifties and sixties and I have a thick skin...I had to. I was determined to get through this for me, and my son's sake, but I had to keep working and earning. Loosing Pat to cancer was devastating but my grieving process would not happen for a few years. I buried myself into my work and new career.

My life was one endless seam of, song and dance routines, with my Sundays off I would go down to Southampton to see my son Aaron. After the show I would go or be lead to actor's haunts like the *Players Theatre* club, *The Arts*, *Groucho's* and various other members clubs. Suddenly being cast off, as a singleton wasn't, too bad after all. Remember I was now in a hit West End musical...we were the toast of London. The fans went crazy during the show they were coming in by the coach loads. On my mother's advice I decided to let my flat out and rent a room in a house near Wimbledon Village. My housemate and landlady was a named Geraldine.

She was very sweet although Geraldine did claim that when I was at her house it was like a knocking shop. I had various liaisons but basically it was a different woman every other night. I often got stopped in the street as people recognised me from the show... it was easy I had my mini dreadlocks I was hard to miss. Even during my solo routine in the show...I swear to you, women would throw their panties on stage. I've seen this during rock gigs I played but not at a top theatre in London's West End. The mind boggles.

But no matter how much I drank, smoked or womanised, the massive hole left in my heart would not be filled. Finally I got busted for drink driving...this was my warning shot. I had to focus on the job in hand and I would now have to get the train to Southampton on Sundays to see my boy. My performance in the *Blues Brothers* caught the attention of several directors one of whom was Michael Rudman another was a BBC director who hired me to act in the dark comedy *Small Metal Jacket*. It was my first and only proper role in a film and it was shot at Bray Studios where the Hammer Horror movies were made. I was also asked to do some voice over work for the film.

I took my son along with me for the voice over session, which consisted of doing military type jargon... however they wanted me to voice a rape scene from the film. Obviously the PA had to take my son off for an ice cream while I did that bit. It was a weird film about female spies in Vietnam dressed as Buddhist nuns who have a weapon inserted into their vagina to seduce and kill the Vietcong. I kid you not!!

Anyway after the end of the *Blues Brothers* run at the Whitehall Theatre I did a series of auditions. I got offered four jobs... one was an avant-garde piece, one was about someone making a quilt in memory of AIDS victims, Michael Rudman's play *Bye Bye Miss American Pie* and *Buddy* the Buddy Holly story. I passed on the first two plays and decided to do Rudman's play for the summer and do *Buddy* in the fall.

My audition for *Buddy* was a foregone conclusion; I knew the assistant director and it was just a standard, textbook, soul performance. My audition for Michael Rudman's play was a bit more complicated. When I turned up they asked me to play a gay West Indian with a French accent who was actually an American! At first - for a micro-second - the cognitive processes receded, however, the memory muscles of my neurological network rebooted. My body and mind assumed an inner focus, by the time they handed me the script I was that character.

You know we all have days where the gods are on our sides and we can literally do anything we are asked to. Well I had one of those days. I did it! Accent and all... plus a great singing audition which blew them away! Well I got the part and it was due to open at the infamous Chichester Festival Theatre during their summer season. I was all sorted now thanks to Michael Rudman. We got on well; two Americans living in Britain...and we shared some of the same pains.

Michael and I had talked about the difficulty of maintaining a relationship being in show business. Well he was married to Felicity Kendall who is kind of British acting royalty and they had two kids but she had an affair with Tom Stoppard the governor of stage & screen plays. Somehow Michael got sacked from Chichester I reckon some powerful figures in the background were behind it. Anyway, however it happened we were not going to do the play.

Michael apologised and actually tried to get me cast in a couple of other productions that never worked out. The only thing about my summer job was that I was already contracted to Chichester Festival Theatre for the job and according to the actor's union they had to pay me!

So I enjoyed three months pay for absolutely nothing...don't you just love it when that happens? I was invited to hang out on the Greek island of Paros for a month with a lady friend. It was my first time in Greece and I loved it. The first time I saw the stars in the Greek sky I was moved to tears. I could understand the inspiration that drove the philosophers,

Rock and Roll and UFOs

scientists and artists to shape such an amazing civilisation.

The end of summer would see me preparing for my third West End show and my second long run working eight shows a week. I was cast to perform in a play with music about Buddy Holly. All twenty-eight actors had to play musical instruments, and they were a very talented bunch of people.

Paul Jury was the music director of the production and Paul Elliot who was executive producer of the show always sported a suntan…like he was always on holiday. He had a string of pantomime shows running through the United Kingdom. Paul Elliot, would always have his shows cast with national and international stars, he was a very influential character in UK theatre.

One thing about signing up for a long running show is that touring with a band is out of the question, so I had to put any work with *Osibisa* on hold. I did manage to squeeze in a couple shows with the band one in Guildford and the other at the Jazz Café with a live album thrown in.

So if you have 'Akra Ka Kra' or 'Osibisa live at the *Jazz Café'* you hear me singing some classic numbers like 'Sunshine Day' and 'Woyayaya'!

Doing a run in the theatre is all about stamina however with a large cast the show really wasn't that taxing. I even managed to learn valve trombone, which was given to me as a prop in the beginning of the show. In all I played guitar, electric bass and trombone in the show, along with dancing and acting.

During a solo spot with two other black singers in the show we managed to bring the house down every night like clockwork. We even received a Buddy award for our performance and I had the honour of playing with the original Crickets! It was during the one thousand performance of the show and Peggy Sue was even there!

A certain trumpet player would come in and play shows in between acting jobs… his name is Colin Salmon. Colin would go on to star in a series of James Bond films and star in many films and television programs. He actually presented us with the Buddy award. And I must say Colin is a humble, nice guy and deserves all the success he has. I enjoyed my time in the *Buddy Holly Story* but I did have problems with the manager of the company. There were a degree of politics within the show but I was above all that because I was not a jobbing actor afraid to lose a gig. Besides they invited me to join the cast based on my reputation from the *Blues Brothers*.

When my time came for contract renewal I informed management that I would not be continuing with the show. I was missing music and wanted to get back to it and little did I know I would be embarking on a new life as a single dad! In the meantime I took my son Aaron on a trip to Los Angeles for a much needed holiday. My mother was so happy to see my son Aaron, she had not seen him since he was a baby. My mum was a busy person… she looked after Leonard

Nimoy's mother-in-law Ann in her capacity as a nurse and she owned a boutique in Riverside about 45 miles from Los Angeles. She stayed with Ann in West Hollywood when she was in Los Angeles, which wasn't far from the Nimoy family residence in Brentwood.

Sandy Nimoy, Leonard's wife, adored my mum she called her the worlds first feminist and of course mum wasn't the first… but she was a highly independent woman. She always owned her own house so if a man got out of line he had to hit the door then hit the road. Sandy was fond of me as well and invited me and Aaron to stay at the Nimoy family home in Brentwood by this time she and Leonard had divorced. Sandy had two children with Leonard, Adam and Julie. I had met Adam but Julie and her husband Gregg were quite friendly and invited Aaron & I over so he could hang with her son.

I took Aaron to Universal studios and we flew up to San Francisco to see my mate Sedrick. It was a good bonding trip for Aaron and I…so good in fact that when we got back to London he told his aunt that he wanted to stay with his dad. So a few weeks later I received a call from his aunt Pam informing me that she was bringing Aaron to stay with me permanently. It was quite sudden, I was unprepared, but I got a bit of help and support from Judy Miller, Dominic's wife and Ann Marie Gaynor, Mel Gaynor's sister in law. So just a few weeks before Christmas, I became a single, fulltime dad. A life changing experience I embraced with all my heart. I loved being a dad. It was a happy time.

I had been dating a very fit stripper named Jill who had a little boy about four years old. I sometimes looked after her son while she was off working in a foreign country. But the best thing about this lady was the fact that she was a vegetarian.

Being that my doctor had already sworn me off red meat as early as 1987 after a song-writing trip to Belgium where I was given rabbit meat for breakfast. I developed an infection, which led to my doctor's prognosis. All in all regarding my lifestyle change and being vegetarian Jill made it an easy transition for me and she was awesome in bed!

However easy it was for me to become vegetarian I still had to understand the types of food I could eat and make a decent meal. I was generally a terrible cook and Aaron was not a vegetarian so that meant a lot of frozen stuff with microwave French fries…Yuk!! Where as I can appreciate the sumptuous taste of a gourmet meal I have always thought that the concept of food was generally boring. If I did not need it to survive I would happily forgo any culinary delights.

I know this sounds strange coming from a culture steeped in the traditions of soul food. And God knows my grandma & mum were excellent cooks. My grandma always had guests over for Sunday dinner in Memphis…her spaghetti cheese dish was to die for. Meanwhile in Riverside, California my mum fed half the neighbourhood and everyone called her mom. My flat was too small for me and Aaron so I rented it out and Dominic Miller's dad introduced me to an estate agent who found me a nice 2 ½ bedroom flat just down the road from Dominic and Jude's house in Wimbledon.

Chapter 9
Black to Africa

Aaron and I moved into our new home around January 1994. By March I got a call from Teddy Osei saying *Osibisa* was invited to go to Cape Town, South Africa to play some gigs and try to do some grassroots community work. Black people were finally going to be allowed to vote for the first time and Mandela was running for president.

With a bit of a politically active past this was an opportunity I could not pass up. Aaron had been invited to stay over at a friend's house for the three week, spring break. However I ended up staying in Cape Town for seven weeks! Poor Aaron...I told him that I was going to hopefully do some much needed, work socially and culturally. I said black people in South Africa had lived under the dreadful apartheid system and now this was their time for freedom.

If anything should happen to me and I didn't make it back alive he was to know that I was doing something for people who had been oppressed for a long time. He put on a brave face although having lost his mum I know he didn't want to lose his dad as well. We were lucky that he was staying with a good family.

Sometimes an opportunity presents itself for something you have been in training for all your life. You may not even realise it at the time but manifest destiny soon raises its head and you know just what to do. These are the times you put your life on the line and if anything bad happens you are content in the knowledge that you were doing the right thing.

We plant seeds of hope and love hoping one day this will grow into the elemental force of nature felt by the whole of humanity. But we always start small small...remember the giant redwood tree started off as a tiny seedling.

When we arrived in Cape Town we stayed in a place called Fish Hoek it was a conservative Afrikaans type of vibe. Not good. But when the English community of Nord Hook Beach heard that *Osibisa* was in town they organised for us to stay in different homes. They would not hear of us staying in hotels. Their hospitality was amazing!

The first place we played was a squatter camp called Site 5. The word went around Cape Town that *Osibisa* was doing a free gig. Suddenly so many people showed up Black, white, Asian and Coloured. You could feel the potential this fledgling rainbow nation had if all her people could come together as one.

The residents from the squatter camp were so proud that we chose their place to stage our first concert. Most of the people that came from the city to see us play would not have necessarily known about Site 5 and certainly would not have gone there otherwise. It was strange coming all the way from London to introduce South Africans to other South Africans but that's what we do!

Our work was beginning... bringing people together. We created a media, frenzy wherever we went. Cape town was beautiful it reminded me of California especially the malls and the ladies! My first day there I met a gorgeous doctor and got it together with her but that was just the start!

I really enjoyed the drives along mountain road from Nord Hook into Cape Town. Even with my vertigo kicking in... the site of the *Kaikapo* shipwreck below was an awesome spectacle. I even managed to go up to Table Mountain where you would have a clear view of Robbin Island, Nelson Mandela's prison for over 30 years.

We did a lot of radio and press interviews exclaiming our grassroots mission of bringing people together from the disparate communities of Cape Town. We lived in the affluent white area but we hung out in the black and coloured areas. We played all over the city: *The Temple of Music* in Observatory, *The Waterfront*, *The Baxter Theatre* and *Club Mon*treal.

We set up and played one night on a baseball diamond with only the lights from the cars and electrics from a single generator! It wasn't announced... we just started playing and suddenly there were 300 people there! I know it sounds ostentatious and maybe a bit of a bold exercise but we wanted access to the people. This was a random insane gesture that made us heroes to the local populace. Our speculative advances, for our mission in Cape Town was starting to take shape.

The people of Site 5 gave us a party to say thanks for choosing their camp as the venue for our first gig. It was a small crowded house, with a tin roof, the Castle lager was in full flow, and a woman was teaching the children to sing in a back room.

I was starting to get claustrophobic and was about to leave when the people started singing in those beautiful South African harmonies. This literally brought tears to my eyes. Everyone around us was singing... it was absolutely magical. I'll never forget it. Imagine having *Ladysmith Black Mambazo* singing in your kitchen... as the harmonies evoke the primal forces of nature to awake the spirits of the ancestors.

As the build up to the historic elections came everyone was so full of hope, the vibe was something else. Lillian Bron our agent who brought us out to South Africa had invited a student doctor to come to stay in Cape Town. Her name was Sinai and she was Eritrean but lived in Rome, she was beautiful! We got quite friendly and became close, she would slip out of Lillian's house to come and sleep with me at night. It was quite a walk for her along the beach in pitch black, darkness but she did it. When Lillian found out about us she hit the roof then punched me in the face. When I pushed her away from me she called the South African Police and claimed that I hit her. I had witnesses a plenty though and no action was taken against me.

But I cooled it with Sinai afterwards besides there were enough women coming around and I had my choice. There was no point in creating bad blood between Lillian and myself, I had not realised up to that point that she was gay or bi-sexual.

Apparently Lillian had been in the South African press previously for stalking a women and she was known as the shit lady because her main business was selling manure. However she was totally dedicated to the band and Lillian got me some session work while I was there but what a personality!

We were approached by the ANC to play for the elections but we passed on their invitation. It was decided that *Osibisa* should be apolitical publicly and not to be seen favouring any one political party although we may have agreed with them. However when we played our penultimate gigs at the *Baxter Theatre* we invited all the political parties to the gig.

One day I decided to do a solo gig with a couple of the guys in the band at a local restaurant in Nordhook Beach to raise money for my friends at Site 5. The gig was a success and I raised a couple hundred rand for the squatter camp.

As an entertainer I am fortunate to have a job that I love and hopefully this brings joy to the people. It's such an honour to be able to use your status to raise awareness of the suffering of others…that's what it's really all about.

We were invited to a winery in the Stellenbosch, which lies at the foot of the Cape Fold mountain range. It is the primary location in this area of the Western Cape for wine production. We were given a tour of the wine production plant and afterwards we sang a couple African songs. The management then presented us with copious amounts of wine and brandy.

We had a serious party that night I'll tell you… but I won't. Precise it to say I ended up with a screamer that night which annoyed my hosts to no end and rightly so. I changed residences after that night of debauchery… but I'd like to think Afrikaner and Black African relations may, have improved slightly. We were cultural ambassadors for Ghana after all. This honour would be confirmed in months to come by the parliamentary ministers of Ghana.

The closer it got to election day the more black people were out in the street celebrating as we all were. Walking down the street you would hear Zulu war cries meandering amongst the many variants of winds that you could find in Cape Town's meteorological listings. All this was to herald in the new chief of staff. History was made with the election of Nelson Mandela, South Africa's first black president.

December of that same year I found myself in Ghana with *Osibisa* to play a gig, for Panafest, which was a pan African celebration of art, music and dance. Stevie Wonder was there as was *Envogue, Culture, Sounds of Blackness, Ras Kimono* and featured artists from all over Africa. This was my first trip to Ghana and we (Osibisa) were treated like royalty.

Osibisa were a Ghana based band and were cultural icons throughout the African Diaspora. We played at the national stadium complete with dancers, acrobats... it was an exciting show! You may say we held our own against all the other acts... The band was fierce! *Osibisa* proved why they dubbed us the Godfathers of African music that night! After the show still buzzing from the gig I went out and jammed at the some local clubs & brought the house down with some of the guys from the band. I was so excited to be in Ghana... I had to share that excitement through music.

It was so special to me because I had been performing in OSIBISA for more than ten years at that point. I felt Ghana was my home as well. I remember Daku Potato, Osibisa percussionist, taking me through the back streets of Accra showing me his old neighbourhood.

Winding through musty smelling back allies near the Makola Market we drifted towards the famed shopping district, which is not far from the Kwame Nkrumah Memorial Park. This thriving market place was the heartbeat of the city where you could find an array of products from car parts to land snails!

I even met his auntie who was quite animated for her plus ninety years. She had been one of the many female traders who dominated the Makola Market. Looking at his relatives I could see a strong resemblance to my own family. I always felt Potato looked like my Uncle Robert but seeing his family just confirmed my paternal thoughts.

Potato was a Ga and his people were fishermen so he was a pretty good swimmer. He was our Buddah, our prophet, our percussionist and our Juju dancer. He could not read books but he could read people and always had a wad of cash on him. Never had a bank account but Potato was easily the most popular member of the band.

There would always be a crowd of women around Potato where ever we played be it Europe or Asia. It was refreshing to see women wanting to be with this man not based on his bank but on his talent. For a moment the bonds that holds us to the treadmill of an enigmatic deity breaks free and we are allowed to celebrate the rhythm of life.

Although Ghana was a poor country with an abundance of natural resources foreign investments were starting to come. A burgeoning middle class was starting to emerge. Ghanaian teachers were known to be excellent educators and many were employed to teach in neighbouring Nigeria. Ghana is known to be one of the most stable democracies in West Africa.

Rock and Roll and UFOs

When I got back to London I got a phone call saying my mum was in a coma and that she was brain dead… It was just after Christmas. Dominic Millers dad Barney bought me a plane ticket with his air miles and Aaron went to stay with Dominic's family. I was devastated upon my arrival to Los Angeles. My brother AJ picked me up and we went straight to the hospital. My sister Rene was there massaging Mum's feet in tears.

The doctor who had attended Kings College in London said there was no hope but as I pleaded to Mum to give me a sign she could hear me… it was obvious that she was indeed brain dead. However just before we left the hospital I saw a tear run down the side of Mum's face. Full of hope I told the doctor and he replied that it was an involuntary body function and that she would not recover.

Just hours after returning to our family house in Riverside, California, we got the call that Mum was pronounced dead. About ten minutes after that call I got a call from Ghana saying that Potato had died in Accra. My only consolation was that I knew Potato would be there, in the great beyond, to greet my Mum.

My path and beliefs detour from the religious to that of a spiritual constitution. The conscious revelations from the cosmos, placates intuitive bursts of inspirations that maintains that inner spark of eternal energy. The spiritual essence gives life to our corporal entity and creates a spiritual source beyond the realm of infinity. What is matter? What is dark matter? What is consciousness? Its all beyond our mode of existence but I believe….

My mother's funeral was a huge affair with relatives and friends flying in from all parts of the country. My Cousin Ann, her daughter Sis flew in from Memphis other relatives came from Boston, Florida, Alaska and of course the multitude of people my mother helped over the years.

It amazed me that a woman with nine children could still help others and make an impact on so many people. It was a sad affair but we celebrated Moms life… my brother Anthony performed some music and I played a CD of a song I had recorded for the funeral.

It was one of my best ever compositions, our youngest brother AJ performed a beautiful rap on the song and I did the vocals. The recording mysteriously disappeared however and was never to be heard again. I can't remember the song… so it's gone forever. Maybe it's better that way.

While we were burying my mother in California Potato was being given the equivalent of a state funeral in Ghana. We had just played a successful show at Panafest in Accra, so Osibisa'a currency was at a very high point, with our popularity gaining near legendary status.

The momentum of the band carried on through to a huge funeral procession for Potato led by Mac Tontoh one of the founding members of the band. I didn't make Potato's funeral in Ghana but we had a fantastic memorial celebration for the Black Buddah in London. Everyone was dressed in the traditional Ghana funeral attire, which gave the drab community hall in

Stonebridge a sudden burst with colour.

The funeral dress consisted of material wrapped around the body to form a type of robe fashion worn with heavy leathered sandals that made a thud when thrown to the ground. Of course, my sandals had plastic soles, which did not have the same thud as the African sandals, but I looked stately in my black garb none the less.

We resembled the apostles, Jesus Christ's disciples, as we stood resplendent in the multi coloured African materials. It was an honour for me to be given a seat a the table with elders as the traditional Ga service proceeded. Libations were poured, prayers were offered, music was made. We had an incredible jam session that night in memory of my old friend and colleague Daku Potato.

Not long…maybe just weeks after the memorial I was singing 'Welcome Home' with Osibisa in Thessalonica, Greece and I thought of my mum and Potato…as I poured my heart into that song…. I held back the silent tears although the feeling was incredible… like an epiphany.

The music bringing forth the spiritual essences of our loved ones within the construct of the universe is a mystery, experienced by many. This song was filmed by Greek TV which you can see on You tube. Just google Welcome Home

Our next big event for Osibisa was a small tour of America and Canada where we played the Toronto Jazz Festival and the Summer Stage in New York's Central Park. New York is one of my favourite places in the world and we had over twenty thousand people at the gig. The bill was Femi Kuti, Osibisa and Baaba Maal headlining. This was at a time when Senegalese artists such as Youssou Ndour were blazing a trail through American high culture and popular music.

Although I think Femi Kuti should have been headlining. BAABA MAAL was Island Records golden boy wonder…a griot of the highest order like Youssou Ndour. The griots of Senegal & Mali sang the history and aspirations of the tribe which is expressed through the most amazing melodic overtones.

Some griots are praise singers but the great ones sing of historic tales and songs to invoke the indelible spirit of the people… with mesmerising effect. The introverted subtle and rhythmic style of Baaba Maal was great but the energy of their show was on a different level.

However with the sunshine and party atmosphere in the crowd it was the strong Afro-beat rhythms of OSIBISA and FEMI KUTI OVER that the people really felt. I will say Baaba Maal was generous and is a fan of Osibisa. He had remembered Osibisa's ill fated trip to his home town in Dakar Senegal. The tickets prices, to see the band, were to high for the local Senegalese people and a riot happened.

The young Senegalese boys blamed the white promoters and started stoning cars and tearing down the fences at the venue. Sol Amarfio the drummer and a roadie almost died when they got separated from the bands motorcade and their car veered into a hostile crowd of stone throwing youths. As you can see touring can be dangerous! Its not all sex and drugs and roll and roll.

I love bringing music to the masses but I love being at home and being a dad I missed my son Aaron when I was on the road. It was a fulltime job… cooking, cleaning, washing, shopping and ironing were just some of the chores I had to deal with. Musicians also have to practice as well! Every night I would pick up my guitar and play songs… singing softly so as not to disturb my neighbours.

Teddy Osei called one day and asked if I would come and record a couple songs for a new Osibisa studio album, entitled Monsore. I wrote two songs for the album with Teddy Osei, which marked my first official writing credit for Osibisa.

I had written a song called 'Lion's Walk' on the last studio album about eight years previously but did not get credited for it. I kicked up a big fuss with Mac Tontoh at the time because I had taken the song to him originally.

It was he who should have put my name on the song…no actually… I should have registered it with PRS or ASCAP. Never wait for people to register your own song… it rarely happens even if you are credited with your works.

Sometimes if you do things with a pure heart and you have the intelligence to know your rights… things generally pan out in your favour. We finished the new Osibisa studio album called 'Monsore' I sang on three tracks for that album. I couldn't rest on my laurels though as I had been offered film work for the BBC! It was a film about African American soldiers in Britain during World War 2.

My second film for the BBC and I'm playing a soldier yet again. But it was going to be about seven weeks work… I was a glorified extra but on the Actors Equity union pay rates. Their were ten of us Black actors who were to shadow the lead actors which included Courtney Vance (The Preachers Wife) who has an affair with a local British woman played by Kerry Fox of 'Shallow Grave' fame.

We had a week of army training and three weeks filming with a month break then three more weeks filming. The other Black actors thought that I should be the union steward… I proved to be too good at my job and will probably never work for the BBC again.

We ended up getting more pay when we weren't called on the film set. As we would be stuck at the hotel all day I managed to get us per dium, which is money per day for food and drink. Touring musicians will be very familiar with the term.

During the break before the next filming schedule I had a short tour with Osibisa booked to play in the states and I had a private audition for a new West End show, it was a cameo role so easy peasy. The show was a rock opera called 'TOMMY' by The Who. And…I got the part!

So I had to get another au pair in to help with Aaron... but all this was possible... at least I had work!

The film, which was called 'The Affair', had been shot in many locations around Norfolk and Suffolk. It was a very picturesque part of England with lots of wooded areas, farms and coastal communities. The terrain is generally flat and very fertile with the odd Viking ship still waiting to be discovered in one of Suffolk's secret inlets.

This was the site of Briton's first capital Roman city Colchester and one of the many settlements for the Norwegian invaders of which many of the local population are descended. The famed warrior queen Boadicea is said to have come from this location and probably travelled the Colchester Road when she marched against the Romans in ancient Londinium.

As the movie was a period piece we had loads of extras for the civilian scenes and I must say, the women looked extraordinary dressed up in their costumes from the 1940s. They were all quite friendly and we flirted a lot during that last dash of summer heat waiting for the autumnal rush.

We got additional soldiers as extras from Mildenhall and Lakenheath US military bases... sometimes up to 200 or 300 men. Bill Nun and Ned Beatty had cameo roles in the film and Harry Belafonte was a producer on the film. It was quite a site to behold on days we filmed all the military vehicles and soldiers marching in a cavalcade amid the heat and dust in the Norfolk landscape.

Bill Nunn had a great vibe... he found out I sang with Osibisa and to my surprise he brought an African drum to the set. I always had my guitar in my dressing room so we jammed on African music and jazz tunes, in between film takes.

I must say it was a fantastic feeling to make a film with a bunch of black actors in Britain for the BBC and HBO! The core ten of us black actors, which included Shakespearean actor Adrian Lester, would stay in touch over the years.

Just before rehearsals started for 'TOMMY' I got a call from a music manager called Nyrone he said, 'Simon Cowell was doing a various artists album with legendary producers Stock and Aitken, and would I like to do one of the tracks for the album?'

I knew Simon from the A&R department of BMG/RCA Records. Label president Harry Magee his boss was the art director on my first single 'Baby Talk'. This was way before American Idol and X-factor although... Simon is now Harry's boss in one of his myriad of companies.

The producers previously had a string of hits under the name of Stock, Aitkin and Waterman. Stock and Aitkin being the talent behind the trio were the producers on this project. I was to learn a cover by Oleta Adam's entitled 'Get Here if you can'.

This song worked well with the type of dance treatment these producers were known for. Their studio not far from the famous Globe Theatre was a technological fantasy. Decked in the latest digital technology of the time the control room resembled the deck of the star ship Enterprise. It was a great session and Mike Stock was very pleasant to work with. So I guess I owe Simon one as this project sort of got me back in the music business.

Nyrone came back to me with another project… to record some music from the Philadelphia soul sound period. The Ojays, McFadden and Whitehead, Teddy Pendergrass were just a couple of the artists who emerged from the Philly sound.

After recording the likes of 'Ain't No Stopping Us Now' 'Love Train' and 'Bad Luck' with a little help from my mate T-Bone from Sounds of Blackness, I put a Philly soul show together. The show was choreographed by Floyd Pearce of British dance troupe Hot Gossip who had made many appearances on Top of the Pops… the British chart show.

Floyd was a brilliant choreographer and at one time I think we had about 20 girls in rehearsals. Although I only used two dancers on shows the routines actually looked great with lots of dancers. One of the performances was for Rubber Ron's Club Submission this was for the S&M and fetish crowd.

Needless to say in between sets I stayed in the manager's office although I did take a walk through the club to see the ladies dressed as dominatrix with fishnets and whips and the guys in weird furry costumes!

In order to work in the entertainment business consistently you have to stay busy and get as many projects in your diary as possible. Which means a lot of hustle and networking by phone or in person. My diary was full right up to rehearsals for **TOMMY**… I was good…I was very good.

Chapter 10
Rock Opera

My cameo part as the Specialist in TOMMY was a part played by Jack Nicholson in the film. However I had to sing this operatic piece as opposed to talk singing, which, Jack did. They were a young cast although there were, a few more mature actors like myself around.

Kim Wilde played Tommy's mother and we got on like a house on fire. We were forever flirting she even told her famous dad Marty Wild that we were engaged just to wind him up. Pete Townsend made all the rehearsals with director Des McAnuff and often told me of the gigs he had planned for John Rabbit Bundrick the keyboard player with The Who.

Pete was very generous and gave many cast parties where we would have open microphone sessions. I was usually made the liaison between the actors and the musicians to organise what the repertoire would be.

Depending on the size of the venue Pete would usually drop £30k-£60k behind the bar to cover food and drink. Whenever there was a birthday a bouquet of flowers would be waiting for you at the stage door… it didn't matter whether you were cast or crew.

Yes Pete Townsend was a good guy to work for. During rehearsals I would join in on some of the group dance routines just to stave off boredom. Wayne Cilento the choreographer clocked me one day during a routine and said, 'You're in', which was fine with me.

I was happy to be working with such a great bunch of people, I had my son living with me… life was good. Although I was seeing different ladies at the time I had not met the one yet.

One thing that actors have to do occasionally is to hob nob during after show parties which are given at the theatre by the ticket agencies. They are the life, line of the theatre. It was during one of these after show parties that I met Soraya. She worked for a ticket agency in corporate hospitality.

It was a classic love story because once our eyes locked on each other… that was it! Soraya had been just the woman I needed at that time, my son Aaron got on really well with her. She was cool, calm, collected and her mum had Irish roots. She grew up in Glasgow Scotland and her dad was a black African from Tanzania. We got married almost a year and a half later and soon after she gave birth to my second son Nkosi Olivier Brown.

Whilst still performing in Tommy. I was approached by an old friend George Stone to help produce segments of a, music television program, that was aired in Nigeria. And sponsored by British and American Tobacco.

I was against tobacco sponsorship however there was so little money in this type of broadcasting I just had to go with the opportunity. My job was to set up and interview artists as well as covering events that would be of interest to the market in Nigeria.

One exciting interview was with Lauryn Hill from the Fugees. I was invited to join her entourage in Kenya to document their fact-finding mission on refugee camps in Rwanda, Tanzania, Uganda and Kenya. Lauryn's dad Mal was there and we got on like a house on fire.

Lauryn was as intelligent as she was talented and her talent knew no bounds. I remember calling her in New Jersey when she was recording the multi Grammy awarded album the Mis-education of Lauryn Hill, she was right in the middle of a vocal take.

Her voice, as I heard it through the telephone, had a supernatural tone about it. You know that feeling you get when you have witnessed something amazing and the hairs stand up on the back of your neck? Well this is what I'm talking about, it was unearthly but in a good way. In Kenya Lauryn had brought a guitar with her as she was learning how to play and I showed her a few chords.

She went to meet some local artists and community leaders, and of course everyone wanted to hear her sing. She turned to me and asked me if I would accompany her on her global hit 'Killing me softly' I figured out the chords… we played the song and also 'A long time coming' by Sam Cook. The crowd loved it!

Her team would split up with half, including my co-producer, going to Rwanda and Tanzania and I would join the rest of Lauryn's crew and her dad on a drive from Nairobi, Kenya to Kampala, Uganda. The drive through the Kenyan highlands was amazing although interspersed with the awesome sight of the Maasai warriors herding sheep and cattle. They are allowed freedom to pass borders in east Africa without passport or identity papers a tradition probably hundreds of years old

We stopped at the Rift Valley site, where remains of the oldest human on the planet was found. It was an incredible sight even with my vertigo kicking in. At one point during the drive I was admiring what I thought were lakes but Mal said they were clouds…we were that high up!

By the time we crossed into Uganda there was a marked difference as the vegetation was very lush...it was so green. Passing the schools in the bush where student's uniform shirts were pink, lime green or sky blue were a marked contrast against the Ugandan landscape. The journey took two days spending one night in El Doret in the Sirikwa area of Kenya.

Upon reaching the hotel we checked in promptly then visited a school on the outside of Kampala. While we were there the National Dance Company requested the company of Lauryn and her entourage to attend a command performance as requested by the president of Uganda.

After an amazing performance the dance troupe asked Lauryn to sing a song so she gave me her guitar and I launched into 'Where is the Love' and Lauryn did an amazing rap directed exactly to those kids in the dance company...she brought the house down.

It was an amazing adventure and I got paid for it and I got to sing and play music with one of America's finest artists. I communed with the beauty of nature in the diverse East African landscape. Upon reflection the poverty we witnessed was sad compared to the abundance of natural resources in those areas' Africa is not a poor continent the people are kept poor by the western corporate interests. I pray that this scenario changes in the future.

By this time I had left the cast of TOMMY to focus on the TV work I was producing as well the many recording sessions I was getting booked for. I went to Nigeria to cover The Kicking in Kano festival in the North of the country. Kano, a desert city, is in the Muslim part of Nigeria, it was safe...almost too safe... not like today with Boku Haram running rampant.

The festival had many of the popular artists performing including Femi Kuti, Lagbadja, Pasuma Wonder and old pal Ras Kimono. I did the interviews on all the artists. The host of the show was a chap called Dr Stewart, who had never been to Nigeria although his image would be super imposed on the stage during performances in the past. It was new technology back in 1997 with edit box you could even change the colour of his shirt.

Unfortunately George Stone and I fell out in Nigeria and I lost my job just before my marriage to Soraya. It was a rough time financially but we managed and along with local gigs... Osibisa also came through with the odd gig and I managed to get some session work. I got an opportunity to do a little TV work with the South African Broadcasting Company filming, editing and compiling programmes. Most of that work was unpaid but what I learned got me work in the future.

Technology was changing in TV, radio, telecommunications, film and music. One day I was approached by a lady, whose friend was looking for backing, for a project, called Napster. I was not comfortable with the idea of this new technology downloading songs off the Internet.

I had used the Internet quite extensively for research on artists I wanted to interview. George Stone would only communicate with me through the Internet as no mistakes could be made through communicating on email as it was written down.

Rock and Roll and UFOs

But all that is academic now as we all know just a few years later the internet would rip the heart out of the music business which is only now just barely finding its feet in the industry. Two events marked the end of 1997 one was the death of Princess Diana and the other was the birth of my second son. When the news flashed about the death of Diana I was on my way to LA to do a gig with Osibisa.

I was only in LA for 3 days so I didn't have time to visit my family but the promoters were friends of mine. Meredith Beale was one of the promoters... I used to jam with him back when I lived in LA and my old friend Remi Kabaka played talking drum with Osibisa. Remi was well known in London and LA he was a legendary figure known for his prowess on percussion and we were also the rhythm section for the Nigerian Independence album I recorded with Martha Ulato back in 1985.

However I did get to do some shopping and I bought loads of baby clothes....by this time Soraya and I knew we were going to have a boy. Having another child made me conscious of the need to make a change in my career in order to look after my family.

The next two years would be a challenge but I was determined to make that change.

In 1999 I got a call to do a session with an Italian producer based in London who lived just down the road from our new flat in Wimbledon. I was recommended by an American producer I had done a bit of session work for as a singer. The Italian producer recommended me to some producers based in Milan.

In December of that year I was invited to Italy to make a solo album of my favourite Osibisa songs... we called the album Osibisa Collection and I got paid a nice wage for the work so that was Christmas sorted.

Soraya introduced me to an old friend whose husband wanted a trailer made for a potential health channel. I made the trailer and Saj liked my work so he asked me to put together a video suite for one his companies, which was fitness centres for women. This was a unique opportunity to research and get more of an understanding of the changing technology in video and film production.

I started getting more work making music videos and documentaries. I made a documentary about Lennox Lewis the Heavy Weight Champion of the World for a company and afterwards I got an offer to make my own music program for ZEE TV the Asian Network. It was a great experience but although I made some really good programs there were a couple of real disasters due to the fact of losing my facilities team and eventually my presenter.

However it was a learning curve and I brought in some great interviews with some legendary artists. The show, called World Spirit was essentially a world music program featuring music videos, performances and interviews. I used my personal contacts to get some amazing artists on my show including: Herbie Hancock, Salif Keita (Mali), Youssou N'Dour (Senegal) with the London Philharmonic, Zakir Hussein (India), Eleftheria Arvanitaki (Greece), Amadou and

Miriam (Mali) and The Sounds of Blackness (USA).

World Spirit featured a diverse selection of artists and it was a great experience for me to be executive producer, researcher, cameraman, presenter and scriptwriter. Sometimes you have to watch what you ask for…you might get it…just hope you are ready for it. My next job ventured into the world of marketing getting celebrity branding for a CD of music for babies called a Baby CD. This job was for Disky Records a subsidiary of EMI Records.

The Baby CD was made by a Dutch composer Raymond Lap and would have a tranquil affect on the babies it was played to. As a father I could attest to the benefits of this music and its positive affect on babies & toddlers. All I needed now was to consult my phone book for contacts for the many celebrities with babies with whom I had worked.

Well besides a good compliment of female British actresses and presenters I managed to get support for the Baby CD from my old friends Kim Wilde, Lauryn Hill and even Victoria Beckham (Posh Spice)! But the masterstroke was getting it mentioned on breakfast TV in Britain. However sometimes if you are too good at your job you are a threat to your colleagues.

As I have learned in the past people will go out of their way to sabotage your work or your influence when they feel their job is threatened. However being a positive person I tend to over look peoples jealous nature. I figure we are all in this together so why not help each other. Sadly and its happened time and time again… people generally in the work place don't see you as an ally but as a threat to their position.

Sadly I fell out with management and left the company however they do say that when one door closes a myriad of doors will open. My life path was stretching before me. Very soon everything I believed in would be questioned, my strength would be tested, as would be the loyalty of friends and colleagues. My old devils would come back to haunt me while on a mission of goodness.

London was in the grips of a tragedy that befell a young Nigerian aged ten years who had been stabbed in the leg and bled to death. It was a sad situation. I got a call from a black community newspaper called *The Voice*, they asked if I would produce a charity song in memory of Damilola Taylor, the young lad who had been stabbed.

Having witnessed the failure of so many charity record projects I declined the offer. Then a channel on the Sky Network asked me to cover Damilola Taylor's funeral and get interviews from the celebrities and politicians who would be in attendance. To make a good film about this young boy who wanted to grow up to be a lawyer so he could best serve his community was maybe the best way to keep the awareness of what happened to him in the public domain.

I took the job and organised my crew which consisted of my editor & cameraman Jack Lecouer, production assistant Marilena Dyranis-Maounis and my son Aaron on sound. I had access to the funeral home where Damilola's body was interred. No other broadcaster had that access. So we went to film them bringing the body out...then it hit me!

In this white casket lay the body of a ten year old boy...what about his mother? What about his father? How they must feel. I was overcome with so much grief that I had to excuse myself while my crew got on with it. It was then that I pledged to myself that I would do a song for Damilola Taylor.

It took a couple weeks to get the film of Damilola finished but I did it and the station was happy. However, more importantly Damilola Taylor's family liked the film. A meeting was setup for me to meet Damilola's father Mr Richard Taylor. He was a fine figure of a man, tall, stately but you could see the indelible hurt on his face. No parent should ever have to bury their own child.

I told Mr Taylor of my plan to make a record in honour of his son and hopefully the charitable trust set up in Dami's name would make money from this. I did not have a clue how I was going to accomplish this monumental task but I had already envisioned the success of this record and that was a good start!

I had a song demoed years ago that I used to sing live, it was called 'Wake up the Morning'. My friend Scott English who wrote a hit called 'Mandy' for Barry Manilow said it was one of the best songs he'd heard in years. I felt the song was appropriate and conveyed the right sentiment.

My first born son Aaron had recently been attacked on the train twice once by a group of black teens and then by a group of white teens. I always thought by having a mixed race child it would help heal the racial divide not compel attacks from the status quo. I felt someone needed to do something to galvanise the community. Everyone was upset by this tragedy black, white, brown Asian or whatever everyone has children that they love and want safe.

As the spearhead of the project I needed someone to act as a steward for the production of the song someone I could trust and with impeccable music and programming skills. Frank Tontoh was Craig David's musical director and had a network of serious musicians and singers at his fingertips. I've known Frank since he 16 when he played in Osibisa. Frank and jazz legend Courtney Pine went to school together and Courtney used to hang out over Franks house all the time practicing their jazz chops.

Frank was the obvious choice... if he had the time. Initially I had a meeting with him and he loved the song and immediately set about making a list as to who could play on the record. I would start making calls as to who to get to sing on the record. One person on the top of my list was Des'ree whom I had interviewed for the Golden Tones TV program in Nigeria. She was a very nice lady and conscious of the troubles in the black community.

I got in touch and she agreed to do it... next on my list was Gabriele whom I had never met but after hearing Des'ree was on board she was up for it. I find it was so important to have, these, successful black woman, as the first artists named for the project. It is a well-known fact that black women are the backbone of the black community.

However it was not just the black community that were devastated by this tragedy and the help and response I got from all quarters of the community was inspiring. The next act I got was Roachford who really stepped up and helped with remixes and he added Damilola's name to the chorus, which worked perfectly. I pulled in Courtney Pine and also British singing group Damage. Damage was being looked after by Max Clifford who had the most powerful PR firm in the UK at the time.

When Max offered his services to the project I knew we stood a better chance of success. All Max had to do was to make one call and the world's press would be at your feet. Next I needed studio time and the best place for this calibre project was Sarm Studios Basing St Notting Hill. I arranged a meeting with the infamous producer and studio owner Trevor Horn who agreed to give us studio time to record the track and do a mix.

The day of the vocal session had arrived. Des'ree, Gabriele, Damage and Courtney Pine were all due to come in and do their parts. As Max had promised, the world's press was there. Mr Taylor, Damilola's father, posed for pictures with students from his son's school along with Des'ree, Gabriele, Damage and members of Craig David's band who played on the record.

Every network in Britain ran this story and the pictures. It felt as if the whole of London was behind the project, which kept the awareness of the tragedy that befell young Damilola Taylor in the public's eye.

With the single 'Wake up the Morning' recorded the next step was to get a deal for its release which I arranged with a local London label with distribution through Universal Music. This sounded good on paper so I arranged a record launch to be held on October 10th 2001.

Having secured most of the artists I had a meet with the group Damage who had sang on the record. After the meeting I made my way to Camden Town tube station. I thought I heard a scream... then the guy at the news stand next to the station announced that one of the twin Towers in New York had been hit by a passenger jet! It was September 11th a date that no one would ever forget.

When I got home I saw on the news that the other tower had been hit by another passenger jet...It was starting to be obvious that this was a devastating terrorist attack that would change the way we live our lives from that day on.

Everyone was in shock for days, as was I but I had to focus on the record launch for the sake of the Damilola Taylor Trust. At a meeting with Max Clifford's office we planned the press coverage for the launch event. I had to admit it was looking good I had national and international stars for the event including Finley Quaye, Des'ree, The Dhol Drummers, Courtney Pine, Osibisa, Gabriele, Roachford and Damage.

The Jazz Café in London was sold out! The launch was a huge success and we raised £1500 pounds from the event. Mr Taylor told me to use the money to make a tribute album. I reluctantly said yes. This project had taken over my life and dealing with middle men in the music industry was difficult. It took me two years to finally compile and record some original tracks.

When I put the call out for artists to contribute to the Damilola Taylor Tribute album the response was enormous. I had more than enough tracks for the album this took about a year… but obtaining the releases from the record companies took a further year! Even though all the artists had already contributed songs to the project the legal departments really dragged out the process.

Getting a release date for the album was stifled because Muff Winwood who had assured me that Sony would release the album, suddenly pulled out of the deal and that left me in the lurch. I was obsessed with making this album a success for the Trust so much so I seriously neglected my own family.

My wife Soraya thought I was crazy and rightfully so. We separated for the 2 years while I worked on the Damilola Tribute album. My life was crazy doing pub gigs every other night in between touring with Osibisa and working on the tribute album by day. My obsession with this project took me to some dark places and I felt so all alone at times. The mantra going round and round in my head was that 'if this project saved just one life it would have been worth my sacrifices.'

But the thing that happened to Damilola should not have happened…a boy coming back from a library getting stabbed and bleeding to death. When I felt the depression kicking in and the anxiety tickling my brain that disembodied voice inside my head would say you are not alone. I had a vast network of artists who contributed and believed I could make this happen. There was strong support from, the London community. I was not about to give up because Sony pulled out.

I contacted an old friend Julius Just who had worked on the World Music Awards in Monaco for years. He in turn introduced me to Amber Callender who had worked in marketing and promotion for the music industry. She came up with the excellent idea of releasing it through a newspaper as a cover-mount CD. It made sense, as it was the newspapers that helped to drive the story of Damilola Taylor.

However I got a call from Mr Richard Taylor informing me to watch my back as Amber had contacted someone in the trust and they were trying to steal the project from me. Imagine my horror when I was told this…two years of hard painstaking work and someone is trying steal the project.

Lucky for me dealing with major artists and major records companies is a complicated business. The labels would not deal with Amber as I had done all the legal work to secure both the releases and the artists and everything was in my name. So Amber had to deal with me.

Rightly so I refused to even speak to Amber Callender after this episode.

I just dealt with the production company, who would manufacture the CD for the Evening Standard Newspaper who agreed to release the CD on the third anniversary of Damilola's death and the Trust would be paid one hundred thousand pounds! I was in tears when I finally signed the agreement between the newspaper, the trust and myself.

Epilogue
A Better World

My victory was twofold...firstly, on the one hand it was nice to know that Mr Taylor had my back and secondly to finally accomplish something that took so much heartache and so much time was not just a blessing for me it was blessing for the community of London. After all the articles written about black on black crime and the plight of lost black boys in the UK education system, there was a tiny glimmer of hope that we the people could come together and sort out the wrongs in our community.

That fact that young black men were becoming victims of senseless gun violence outraged and frightened many people. I have three black sons and I felt the anxiety that many parents must have felt. The more I appeared at black community events the more I realised how disjointed the black community really was. Many more people from the black community could have come forward, however I am pleased with the ones that stood up both black and white.

My religion is people...I have studied and observed many religions and the only thing that adds to the chaos are the people involved. Spirituality has to be the key. That is where you will find your deity...in the heart of every person with a spiritual aptitude. There is good and bad power in the consciousness of the people so we have to harness that goodness and keep the balance with the negative energy. Ying and yang are the natural forces of the universe and one can't exist without the other.

Today, with technology invading every aspect of our plane of existence... the balance of power is unstable and it seems like the devil is winning. That is why it is important to stand up when you see wrong being perpetrated. Your voice will just be one of many who feel as you do. This is what happened when I took that first crucial step to try and galvanize the community and keep the awareness of what happened to Damilola in the public arena.

After years of working on the project for the trust I was finally invited to the opening of the Damilola Taylor Centre in Peckham South East London where I presented the wife of Prime Minister Tony Blair a copy of the Damilola Taylor Tribute CD featuring Robbie Williams, The Gorillaz, Craig David, Courtney Pine, Gabriele, Ms Dynamite, Blue, Sting, So solid Crew, Des'ree, Mis-Teeq and Liberty X.

Soraya and I got back together although it was never the same... even though we would eventually have another beautiful son named Otto. I would go back to university and get my masters degree plus a teaching certificate to start teaching but nothing worked for her. We would get separated and divorced some four years later.

Sometimes in life you have to face perils alone even when you have a lot of support from people... but the frustrations, setbacks, forgotten promises, deceit and lies you have to confront and deal with yourself. I can be as insecure as the next artist but those two years working on the album had its high points. However there were more lows.

Let me just say I almost had a nervous breakdown.... dealing with and creating with the artists was a pleasure but the record and publishing companies could be challenging at best and some of the manipulative scenarios would have sent a lesser experienced person packing.

Patterns in ones existence are often repeated and once you have blazed your trail then you know the path you should take. If you keep knocking on that door someone will eventually open it even if it's just to keep you from knocking on it again. That's how I can best describe my career in the Entertainment industry. Order amongst chaos, quiet before the storm...focus on the objective don't loose sight of your target.

Get use to rejection, sidestep hangers on, adapt an ohm quality to your being, be at peace with yourself and keep on knocking. You are doing the right thing and the master creator will carry you through.

I knocked on some of the same doors two years later when I released my solo album Gregg Kofi Brown and Friends 'Together as One. This time I got some amazing musicians to work with such as Billy Cobham, Stanley Jordan, Airto, Sting, Eddie Gomez, Des'ree, my ole mate Dominic Miller, Gabriele and the finest session musicians from Italy and the UK.

However by the time my album came out, the Internet with the scourge of free downloading was starting to have a devastating effect on the music industry. It reminded me of my UFO experience, when in my mind's eye I remember seeing the city's world, and looking at each city like an LCD circuit board that would be used to make a transistor radio.

The traffic on the road would be like the energy strips of the circuit board leading to buildings that were like transistor and resistors. Except it was not a circuit board. What my first encounter of the third kind lead me to see was really a computer chip The World on a Computer chip. Sound familiar. Seems like I was being given a glimpse of things to come and I was too dim to work it out until recently; almost 35 years later.

My multiple UFO encounter that night is unexplained but was verified by the Los Angeles Times. Was it aliens? I don't know. Was it trans dimensional beings? I don't know. Was it a military project? I don't know but maybe.

All that is clear to me is at the moment that experience happened, it marked a pivotal point in my own life of what I had accomplished at that time and what I would accomplish in the future. Like a harbinger of what was to come in my life my family, my sons Aaron, Nkosi and Otto, my career in music and theatre, and my academic pursuits.

If you work hard at something and make your presence known to the world… any part of the world, life has a way of directing you to the right path. Its up to you to choose to take that path… its your choice. But you have to be prepared and ready.

ROCK 'N' ROLL AND UFOs

Gregg Kofi Brown has transcended many genres of music...

Rock 'n' Roll and UFOs is an anthology of music from Gregg Kofi Brown's career and contains previous unreleased songs, remixes and demos, with many guest musicians and artists such as Sting guitarist **Dominic Miller**, **Bomb da Bass**, **Osibisa**, the cast of the **Who**'s *Tommy*, The Chimes' **Pauline Henry**, the Who's former keyboard guru **John Rabbit Bundrick** and Seal guitarist **Gus Isidore**.

The CD is a companion to Gregg Kofi Brown's **autobiography** of the same name which covers his early career in Los Angeles and London. From his first pro tour with **Joe Cocker** and **Eric Burdon** to close encounters of a third kind in a California desert and his adventures touring the world with African rock pioneers **Osibisa**. His journey includes starring in hit west end productions in London, recording and touring with infamous rock bands like Hanoi Rocks and the Members.

His first tour in Gambia and Senegal West Africa supporting African superstar **Youssou N'dour** is well documented, as is his work in the African and West Indian music scene in the UK.

The last few years has seen Kofi perform with **Damon Alban's African Express** and collaborate live with **Amadou & Mariam** featuring **Beth Orton**.

CD and book available soon from Gonzo Multimedia

www.gonzmultimedia.co.uk

Gonzo Books

There is still such a thing as alternative Publishing

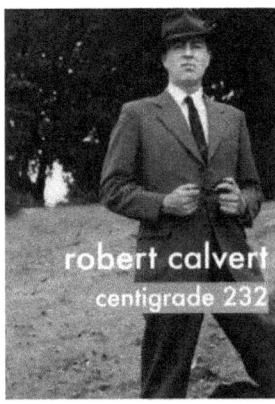  

Robert Newton Calvert: Born 9 March 1945, Died 14 August 1988 after suffering a heart attack. Contributed poetry, lyrics and vocals to legendary space rock band Hawkwind intermittently on five of their most critically acclaimed albums, including Space Ritual (1973), Quark, Strangeness & Charm (1977) and Hawklords (1978). He also recorded a number of solo albums in the mid 1970s. CENTIGRADE 232 was Robert Calvert's first collection of poems.

Hype 'And now, for all you speeding street smarties out there, the one you've all been waiting for, the one that'll pierce your laid back ears, decoke your sinuses, cut clean thru the schlock rock, MOR/crossover, techno flash mind mush. It's the new Number One with a bullet ... with a bullet ... It's Tom, Supernova, Mahler with a pan galactic biggie ...' And the Hype goes on. And on. Hype, an amphetamine hit of a story by Hawkwind collaborator Robert Calvert. Who's been there and made it back again. The debriefing session starts here.

Rick Wakeman is the world's most unusual rock star, a genius who has pushed back the barriers of electronic rock. He has had some of the world's top orchestras perform his music, has owned eight Rolls Royces at one time, and has broken all the rules of composing and horrified his tutors at the Royal College of Music. Yet he has delighted his millions of fans. This frank book, authorised by Wakeman himself, tells the moving tale of his larger than life career.

There are nine Henrys, pur‐ported to be the world's first cloned cartoon charac‐ter. They live in a strange lo fi domestic surrealist world peopled by talking rock buns and elephants on wobbly stilts.

They mooch around in their minimalist universe suffer‐ing from an existential crisis with some genetically modified humour thrown in.

Marty Wilde on Terry Dene: "Whatever happened to Terry becomes a great deal more comprehensible as you read of the callous way in which he was treated by people who should have known better many of whom, frankly, will never know better of the sad little shadows of the past who eased themselves into Terry's life, took everything they could get and, when it seemed that all was lost, quietly left him ... Dan Wood‐ing's book tells it all."

Rick Wakeman: "There have always been certain 'careers' that have fascinated the public, newspapers, and the media in general. Such include musicians, actors, sportsmen, police, and not surprisingly, the people who give the police their employ‐ment: The criminal. For the man in the street, all these careers have one thing in common: they are seemingly beyond both his reach and, in many cases, understanding and as such, his only associ‐ation can be through the media of newspapers or tele‐vision. The police, however, will always require the ser‐vices of the grass, the squealer, the snitch, (call him what you will), in order to assist in their investiga‐tions and arrests; and amaz‐ingly, this is the area that seldom gets written about."

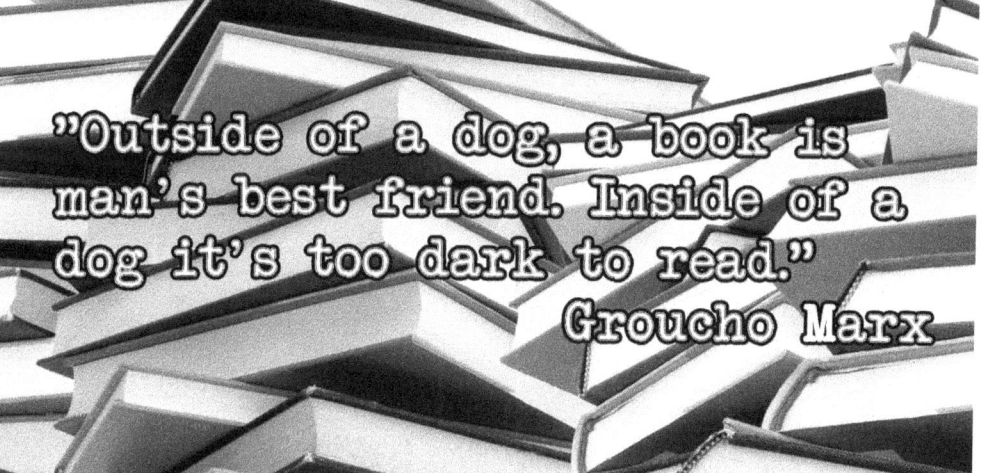

"Outside of a dog, a book is man's best friend. Inside of a dog it's too dark to read." Groucho Marx

Bill Harkleroad joined Captain Beefheart's Magic Band at a time when they were changing from a straight ahead blues band into something completely different. Through the vision of Don Van Vliet (Captain Beefheart) they created a new form of music which many at the time considered atonal and difficult, but which over the years has continued to exert a powerful influence. Beefheart rechristened Harkleroad as Zoot Horn Rollo, and they embarked on recording one of the classic rock albums of all time Trout Mask Replica - a work of unequalled daring and inventiveness.

Politics, paganism and .... Vlad the Impaler. Selected stories from CJ Stone from 2003 to the present. Meet Ivor Coles, a British Tommy killed in action in September 1915, lost, and then found again. Visit Mothers Club in Erdington, the best psychedelic music club in the UK in the '60s. Celebrate Robin Hood's Day and find out what a huckle duckle is. Travel to Stonehenge at the Summer Solstice and carouse with the hippies. Find out what a Ranter is, and why CJ Stone thinks that he's one. Take LSD with Dr Lilly, the psychedelic scientist. Meet a headless soldier or the ghost of Elvis Presley in Gabalfa, Cardiff. Journey to Whitstable, to New York, to Malta and to Transylvania, and to many other places, real and imagined, political and spiritual, transcendent and mundane. As The Independent says, Chris is "The best guide to the underground since Charon ferried dead souls across the Styx."

This is is the first in the highly acclaimed vampire novels of the late Mick Farren. Victor Renquist, a surprisingly urbane and likable leader of a colony of vampires which has existed for centuries in New York is faced with both administrative and emotional problems. And when you are a vampire, administration is not a thing which one takes lightly.

"The person, be it gentleman or lady, who has not pleasure in a good novel, must be intolerably stupid."

Jane Austen